MW00780701

Fresh Peace

Daily Blossoming of the Soul

Fresh Peace

Daily Blossoming of the Soul

Jaiya John

Soul Water Rising

Camarillo, California

Fresh Peace: Daily Blossoming of the Soul

Copyright © 2015 by Jaiya John

All rights reserved under International and Pan-American copyright conventions.

No part of this book may be reproduced or transmitted in any form or by any means electronic or mechanical including photocopying, recording, or by any information storage and retrieval system, without written permission from the publisher, except by a reviewer, who may quote brief passages in a review. Address inquiries to books@soulwater.org.

Printed in the United States of America

Soul Water Rising
Camarillo, California
http://www.soulwater.org

Library of Congress Control Number: 2013921731
ISBN 978-0-9916401-3-3

First Soul Water Rising Edition, Softcover: 2015

Inspirational / Spirituality / Mindfulness / Wellness

Editors:
Jacqueline V. Richmond
Kent W. Mortensen

Book and cover design, and cover photo by Jaiya John

The world,
like an old poet,
gets freshened with soul water
and light rising new with the sun.

—Jalal ad-Din Rumi

AUTHOR'S NOTE

On May 7, 2013, the first emailing of *Fresh Peace: Daily Inspirations* occurred. For years, I had yearned for a way to more broadly and deeply share this fervent spirit river running through my vessel all of my life. Very quickly after the inaugural emailed inspiration, I began to receive expressions of gratitude from many souls. I was touched and further bowed. This reinforced what I have seen in my life and work: that so many of us are starving and thirsty for something that lifts, cleanses, and renews the spirit.

Almost immediately, it became clear to me that *Fresh Peace* would also be shared in book form. This book is the first of what I hope will be an ongoing series, emergent from an ocean of inspiration. Inspiration that flows into me directly from my experiences with the Divine nature of our humanity and our world.

We should be clear here: I am no more than a soul who cares, compelled to share a momentary understanding. Brimming with Love for this Creation, and moved greatly by both our collective suffering and our capacity for healing and goodness, I choose to share. I am no authority and care not to be. I do feel invested in and responsible for contributing what Light I can to this vast and profound field of being human. And so I share. Thank you, really. Thank you for receiving. May Fresh Peace be yours.

She wanted Peace. So she played beautiful music, painted beautiful expressions. It was not enough. She went on long walks. Gave away possessions. Smiled more. Stopped multitasking. Not enough. She bought more reverent clothing. Read spiritual books. Spoke spiritual words. Not enough. She changed her relationships. Attended classes. Cut her hair. Improved her diet. Attended worship. Found a new job. Traveled. Came back. All of it, not enough.

Then, one day, she looked inside herself, the place she had run from all her life. She found two Truths: the concentrated ego of suffering and fear, and the simmering ember of Peace. Realizing that Peace was a seed already inside her, she decided to try something new. She decided to Love more. Herself. Others. All things. In every moment. She opened. The ocean inside came out. The ocean outside came in. She dissolved in two oceans. Became immeasurable Lightness. She found Peace.

Love is the sunlight that awakens the seed of Peace.

W hat a joy to be in a continuous conversation
with Peace. Everything feels lighter, looks
clearer. Your heart purrs along, content. Your body
is loose, relaxed like a ribbon aloft in the breeze.
And your mind is so wide open, like a child
drinking summer rain from the sky. Why would
we ever want any other companion for
sharing thoughts and feelings?

Peace will affirm our every desire and note of
happiness. Peace will encourage us out of
pessimism and gloom. Peace assures us of the
Purpose to our road and its stones and turns. Peace
punctuates the kisses of harmony upon our soul. If
you wish to have the kind of conversation right
now that leaves you feeling so good inside, Peace
is waiting. If you desire a life of ongoing serenity
and clarity, start chatting up Peace and never stop
rambling away.

There are days we wake wanting to pour honeyed water down our throats. Yet the new day gives us only saltwater. Here is where we have a choice. We can lament what is not, or we can become a fish and take advantage of an ocean of provision.

We are never lacking entirely. Only lacking vision of Entirety. Branches weave a lattice outside your morning window. Become a songbird and go in your mind to that playground in the trees. Sing something beautiful into being. Make the world a garden with every breath. Take off your night clothes and spend this day in nakedness. Soul is a nudist and wants to get to the bare heart of things.

Come... warm your hands on the fire that is your soul. It burns for you. Would you let its torrid infatuation have some measure of satisfaction? It would make a good Lover, confirming your truer beauty in countless strokes. It would say to you, *I understand*, each time your torn heart cries for validation. Your soul is there for you, an eternal friend, steadfast Lover, speaker of all you long to hear.

But your ear, your ear is tuned to the world and all its many frantic waving hands saying, *Come this way, we'll show you a real blaze.* You fall in Love with a sweeping fable, and you go its way. When you arrive you discover no fire ever existed there. Nothing resides in that place but cold and damp and hollows. Your fingers freeze and ache. Next, your heart. All your false friends have now fled. You are lost and alone in woods of despair. Shivering and starving, frightened and panicked, you seek shelter for the long night ahead.

But then, Grace. A wondrous glow peeks through the elders. You stagger that way, curious, at your last resolve. Closer, you encounter the truest friend you will ever know. At last you sit and warm your hands on the fire that is your soul.

The leaf on the branch felt safe until the aphid arrived. The aphid felt safe until the ladybug arrived. Ladybug felt safe until the dragonfly. Dragonfly felt safe until the snake. Snake felt safe until the robin. Robin felt safe until the Raven. Raven felt safe until the Raccoon. Raccoon felt safe until the cougar. Cougar felt safe until the human. Human felt safe until the storm. Storm felt safe until the calm. Calm didn't just *feel* safe, it *was* Safety. Nothing could arrive to change that.

Serenity is a sanctuary that never leaves us. It comes with the lease of being human. Breathe yourself in through its window. Stay for a while. Eventually you may grow familiar with the blessings that live in the household we call Peace. If so, you might not want to leave.

Humanity is a dry prairie, waiting. Your Love, a spark. Make fire. Transform this world in beauty. Reduce us to ash in your compassionate flame, so we may be reborn, a gushing garden. Never doubt that you are this influential. We have seen a single soul spread darkness over the earth. And a single soul spread Light. You are a torch of Love. The human wilderness is so very vulnerable to your potential to spread Love's fire.

If your life feels cluttered with meaningless priorities and relations, breathe your Holy breath of Love and watch all illusions turn to dust. Now your life will be a fertile soil and soon enough sacred sprouts will grow. You have the capacity to remake us all, in your image of Light. In your Love. Please, start the fire.

S tructure and order are great for gathering, building, and charting direction. For actually getting there, often it is best to tear down what we have built. This is how Soul projects can be. Continual building up and tearing down, feeding then starving, watering then thirsting. Shining a light, then dashing open the drapery on that space to reveal a still brighter light that consumes the prior.

On we go, erecting, erupting, eradicating, until flocks of veil fill sky, migrating away from us at our behest. Until blindness submits to us, exhausted, and revelation opens a door. We move through that crease and are rewarded with more building up and tearing down. Incremental burials and excavations, forever ascending the immeasurable heights, treading a path of no lines or length.

This is how Soul projects can be. Contracts are bid out to those with a penchant for Peace. And the ultimate reward? Infinite lightness of Being. Shall we begin?

When the water is calm and clear, we see our true face.

When our mind is calm and clear, we see our true nature.

When our heart is calm and clear, we see our true desire.

When our spirit is calm and clear, we see our true calling.

Today, may you choose to be calm and clear. In a life of choices, few choices bring more reward.

*T*o *Love all that has been Created as we would its Creator.* This is our only mission, and our only hope for Peace. And yet even as we claim to be of this or that faith, we resist with every breath opening into the very element that makes any faith worthy: Love. Not partial, portioned, sanctioned, segregated Love. Love unbound and blind to the distinctions of human ego and fear. Love that makes all souls we regard... an aura that cannot be regarded. Except in Love. We have one hope for Peace. Take it. And on this earth, be a creator.

Make Love.

Morning seems to give us a measure of hope for what is to come. A sense of possibility. As though the sand and silt of yesterday and its yesterdays have been kindly washed away. As though our desire and need have been provided a space ahead in which to find their fulfillment. A sweet anticipation lingers in its air. If this is true of morning for you, may you make your entire life a morning of the soul.

If you are going to wake, awaken into your giftedness. And if you are going to plan, plan to release all plans. The taste of freedom is stored in the spice jar of release and surrender.

No bread rises like the bread of faith. So if you are hungry, or you wish to feed your circle of beloved, bake fresh bread in the oven of your soul's belief that you are not the way, just a traveler walking the way... and that the way has been laid and prepared for you.

Moon and sun are circles only because they have been turning. Turn toward Love, Creation's binding force of union, and see yourself become whole, as a circle. No more yearning, except to praise ever more deeply in this garden of Sacredness.

Take away all the things that you fear. What remains is your purpose. What remains is how you would be living if not for your fears. Purpose is not a mystery. It could not be more persistent or redundant in announcing itself to us. We like to lament that if only we could figure out our purpose, our life would change and we would have happiness and Peace. The truth is, one of the things we fear the most is our purpose. And so we join the human gangs of fear ruling the streets of life, and we go in that direction.

If we can focus on *why* we fear what we fear, we can learn new personal ceremonies for burning those fears away. With each fear incinerated, Purpose comes into view. Then the good times begin. Purpose is like a crack in the ceiling, or a cloud formation in the sky. Once we see it, we can't stop seeing it. And a purposeful life is on the way!

Nutmeg is great in tea, or eggnog, or waffles. In your orange juice? Not so much.

So often, we take something good, like our desire, and place it where it doesn't belong. Like inside an insecure impulse. This turns our desire from goodness into self-destruction. If we can learn the art of keeping our desire where it belongs, on a path of surrender and sacredness, we can compose a wonderful recipe that tastes great every time.

Desire doesn't belong in our rivers of self-rejection and doubt. It belongs in the purity of our Divinely-tuned heart and soul. Now that's a recipe for which your family and friends will want the secret.

L ook! Spring is blooming again in your heart. If you haven't noticed, it's not because new beauty isn't there. You simply have been looking in other directions, focusing on other things. Your heart is forever blooming. You can know this by the fragrances of Hope and Joy that overcome you in those moments when you are living close to the river of your soul. When you are declining the false bouquets the world brings to your door, and immersing yourself by the warmth of your true home's fireplace, reading a great book written by your desire.

Today, find something—anything—that makes you smile innocently. Dream of it for the rest of the day. For that one thing is evidence that spring is blooming again in your heart.

If you are wondering why others don't seem to be kind to you as often as you would like, consider the truth that sugar dissolves much more easily in warm water than in cold. No matter how warm you perceive yourself to be, remember, someone's sugar is shivering and hoping you will warm up just a little more.

Be the one in whose presence others lose sight of worries and instead catch the scent of Peace. Don't be the one who brings gifts. Be the one who takes away illusions and blindness. Be the radiance that never wilts, the surrender that never stops bowing down. Be the pearl glimmering in the water, the moon stone in a dark sky. Be the voice of a dove on a night filled with predatory howling. Be the tropical flower growing in the desert, the dry desert breeze comforting a tropical humidity. Be the exception to every cruelty, the caring that stands out as more than what was needed. Be what skin feels at sunrise on a cold morning. Be the freedom of creativity.

And that memory of happiness from a moment of childhood? Be that, too.

Your life is a great bow pulled taut and ready in the hands of God. Through your Love, be the arrow. Pierce the suffering of this world.

Take flight.

Don't blink. Grace is perched on your eyelash, waiting to fall into your vision. It might be best to keep your precious eyes...

wide open.

Read the letter. The one life is writing you. Read it carefully. Be fully present. Empty and unbias your mind. Open your heart and spirit. Read the letter. Memorize it. Then go beyond memory, and internalize the letter. Make it so deep a part of you that you can recite its words, and the words within its words. Fill the spaces between its words with inspiration. Learn the tone and touch and voice of the letter. Its scent and rhythms. Read the letter life is writing you. Read with such passion and devotion that its words disappear and you *become* the letter. Then go out into the world and, like a true master-*peace*... let yourself be read.

Let's make it plain. When we deny our truth, we suffer. When we caress our truth, we heal. If fear and faith are the difference between our suffering and our healing, faith seems like a good investment. Faith that we are capable of healing, because we were capable of hurting in the first place. Our capacity to be hurt is a symptom of our capacity to heal.

Through how much have we healed in this life? Have we not gained any faith from this? Faith that we were made to walk in truth and in doing so, to move through healing? Faith that we are not alone? Faith that a Miracle operates in us just as continuously as our blood flows?

In reality, you are always practicing faith. If you were not, you might be alive, but surely you would not be *living*. Let us deepen our practice, until by virtue of our devotion, we are changed... faithfully.

When we taste something we like, we usually eat more. Strangely, when we taste Peace we often place it back in the pantry. Maybe for some, Peace is an acquired taste. A particular child cannot stand the taste of sweet potatoes. Then she grows up, and behold, she Loves to bake sweet potato pies. Perhaps our first step with Peace is not to acquire its taste, but instead to grow up in spirit. Then Peace might be a taste acquired by our growing up.

Here's to growing, and the higher tastes it brings.

Pilgrimage: a journey to Sacredness.

Is our entire life not a pilgrimage? Our suffering is a yearning for home. We are sea birds wandering the desert, aching for the ocean... aching more deeply when we smell its salt in the air. We are desert tortoises, paddling the ocean, direly needing land and dryness, fantasizing stillness and solidity. And yet the Glory of our life is that we carry within what we came from. We are never away from it.

You are a good example of this. Even when you don't feel beautiful, you are the radiance of Divine beauty. Your heart is going to be just fine. Sometimes it is like a potted plant. All it needs is for you to position it where it can get more sun. And when you feel the call to Sacredness, strip away what is not real from your life, and give yourself to the pilgrimage. You are going that direction anyway.

Morning breeze is like an audition for humankind. It moves the trees, plants, flowers. It ripples water, makes dust dance. Morning breeze moves all other living things. It should move us, too. Next time you feel morning breeze, know that the audition has begun. Prove that you are alive and a part of this Creation. *Be moved.* And when the audition has passed, see that you are now inside another one, for each life moment wants to know what kind of spirit we are bringing to this production. No matter the cast, stage, or script... no matter the size or energy of the audience...

be moved again.

Silence is a siren, calling out for the voice of Sacredness. Grow quiet and let that Pure blanket come over you. Water falls so that you may rise into your state of serenity. Sit by a waterfall and rise into the place where earth worries kiss the reassuring sky. If you want just a little more happiness in your heart today, go somewhere where Creation is singing and join the choir as though you have been a member since the beginning. Because you have been. In fact, you are the choir's original song.

Hold out your hand. Creation is pouring out waterfalls of True blessing. Fill your palm and drink. No need to beg for false drink in markets of hedonism and illusion. Stay away from the hucksters hard selling you sugar water when you can have your fill of sweetwater filtered through Grace. Hold out your hand. What pours from the high mountains called Holiness runs devotedly through streams of your own contemplation to reach this lagoon of now and offer itself to you. It is a never-ending waterfall of all things that soothe your soul. The pouring is all around you, always.

Hold out your hand.

Whatever you want in a pure way... is a seed that has been planted in you. We are not the flowers that arise from our life. We are the soil from which those flowers grow. Let the sunlight of this day have its way with you... all the Loving kindness and Creation beauty you encounter. Allow yourself to be watered by present circumstance, even the challenging parts. Open yourself to the fertilizer of inspiration, joy, pain, and pain's healing blossoms.

If various forms of bees, hummingbirds, and butterflies visit your tender sprouts, begin a relationship. They will return when you in your fruitful seasons have nectar to offer. In other words, whatever arrives to be blessed by your Goodness, make it feel welcome. You are a ground that has been planted with a Pristine desire. What you want in a pure way... is the very indicator of the Purpose of your life. Grow that and be fed abundantly.

Make your soul a sunroom, where you read all the books written by your intrinsic Sacredness. Take down the dreary drapes darkening your reading space. Open the windows and swim in shafts of morning light. Make your sunroom comfortable, with pillows and cushions and incense. But not too comfortable, for this sunroom is not for falling asleep. It is for falling into the brightness of yourself, the part of you whose lineage is Immensity. Stretch out your body in this warm and inviting sanctuary. Your mind and spirit will follow, sweetly moaning themselves awake.

Read all day long, until the industrious ones grow jealous and judge your apparent inactivity. Shoo them away and get lost in your truest activity: reading every word of your soul over and again, savoring the delicacy. Relishing the sun you have invited to roost in your home space, your sunroom constructed to grow leaves of Light.

All of this life is Grace. The sweet bell chime of nature's music. Beauty's infinite faces caught in our glance. Irritation like grain beneath the nail. Impatience struck on a moment's chord. Deep hurt. Euphoric relief. Silence. Chaos. Stillness. Pollution. Purity. Night rainbows. Day shadows. Form. Freedom. Imprisonment. What we taste on the tongue is the mist of another thing not tasted: Grace. What we perceive is the emission of the unperceivable: Grace. What comes to us comes from Grace. What we give goes back to Grace. Here is the purpose of all this living: Grace.

And you... you are a chalice for Grace, a drinker of Grace, and the wine of Grace that blesses both the chalice and the drinker. Be thirsty for the Kindness we have been provided. Search for the last drop in the glass. Lick the bowl. The more you yearn for Grace, the more you become attuned to It. A relationship develops, the intimacy of which becomes the glow by which you are known. Becomes the reason others whisper of you: *I don't know what it is, but she/he just seems to be filled...*

with Grace.

If you cannot manage to become the sun and shine Love's salvation on the world, at least become the moon. Then go and stand near one who is the sun. Reflect her light onto those who cannot sleep, or who simply Love to stroll through heavy shafts of illumination, more awake than ever while all around them, others are wide asleep. Hopefully, after enough time spent reflecting light, you will become light.

Doesn't contagiousness work like this? Whatever your worldly aspirations, have one deeper gift you wish to leave humanity. One goal for your existence that is promised to have a good ending. Devote your life to learning what it means to be Light in the world. Then dare to graduate from student to teacher. Make all other curricula look like dust on the eyelash of the sun.

When rain kisses ground after a long drought, ground plays hard to get. It won't just part its mouth... its lips have grown dry and resistant, so rain runs over that ground and floods away. When Profound Truth tries to bless us after so long living in a dishonest world, how do we treat this end to our inner drought? The easy answer is that we open and drink. But first our ground must soften, or Truth won't sink in. Through our hard-baked resistance, Truth will flood away.

This is where choice comes in. Friend, don't think you haven't been spotted around the fire, peering into the flames. Clearly you desire the secret to burning so brightly. First, try softening by learning a deeper shunning of worldly enticements. Then you will become the pure state that tastes Truth and doesn't spit it out... you, the form dissolved into firelight that lifts for everlasting Sky.

W e are at the most magical swimming hole. It is called, TODAY. You, friend, are standing at the edge of the cliff, considering whether to jump in. Some souls are already swimming below, gleeful and lighthearted. Others are telling you it's too dangerous to jump.

Right now, maybe you could use a push. The most important thing about your life today is not the condition of your body, bank account, or bad circumstances. The most important thing about your life today... is that you have life today. You are standing at the edge of a cliff called Faith and Surrender, blessed with an opportunity to jump into pools of Abundance. But you aren't quite sure. Most other souls wouldn't jump. But you aren't most other souls. Today is the day you take the plunge, descend beneath the blessing waters, and surface to realize that the only danger you ever truly faced in the first place was in what you would have missed had you not jumped.

So, Dear One... jump. And tomorrow, just because you are alive... jump again.

M oon grows fat so it can bless its belly in the sun. Romance can be this way. Life changes continuously because Love is chasing Itself around the gardens of Creation, laughing at how everything transforms at Its touch. We can be in harmony with this magic show, or we can fight change at every turn, holding on and grasping for what cannot be possessed. Why not be the one who thrills at Beauty as It treks from caterpillar, to cocoon, to a carnival of flight? The more joy you show life as it changes, the more life will share its joys with you. Then you too can join Love as it goes running... wild and in Love.

Let our every act and thought be praise for what is Holy. And as all of life is Holy, let our whole life be praise. For what is praise but the porch light we leave on, for our Beloved. The soul bread we bake for Creation's appetite. The way you wake with Love in your eyes. And the parting of your individual self to let in the tide of ALL.

They say you are alone and separate. Break that illusion into a million faces of glass that catch sun's fire and paint the world in Union glow. With your smile, give praise. Cry your praise. Dance your praise. Run your palm over the soft pages of moments that compose the book of your life... and feel the soothing touch and tenor of praise.

If you must smoke, smoke a Peace pipe.

If you must kill, kill your hatred.

If you must get drunk, get drunk on the Truth.

If you want to get high, get high on Grace.

If you choose to be blind, be blind to ugliness.

If you gossip, spread word of someone's goodness.

If you are bored, pick up the mystery that is life and go for it.

If you are going to infect someone, first get sick on the most potent strain of Love.

If you want to see the most incredible thing, open your eyes like you did the first time and see the Beauty that is this world again.

Drink this day like a fine cup of jasmine tea. Mist your face in its pure steam. Sip slowly and be present. Let each drop announce itself on your lips before you swallow. Stir it up gently, with a swirl of passion. Allow its richness to steep and saturate your drink. Hold this day softly in both hands. Cradle it in your affection, swaddle it in attentiveness. Blow tenderly to cool its heat. Feel this day move through you and spread its warmth, a cloud settling a hopeful valley.

When you reach the last tea at the bottom, savor what has gathered there: concentrated sweetness and flavor. And when the drink is done, set down your cup ever so sacredly. For as you sleep, the cup is filling with a brand new day.

O ne journey never ends: BEING. The breath we take is not ours, it is the world's. Our light: the exhalation of Love's infinity. Our body: the tender leaf inside of which Creation gathers. Our lifetime: the branch where ancestors perch to gaze the valley of human ages. Our heart: the sanctuary pool where dream flocks gather to drink their fill and rest their lofty wings.

We are the road and its dust, trees and their sentry, sky and its freedom, earth and its wealth. We are forever turning in the smallest grain, the crystal rain, Wind's ministry, Caring's plains. We can breathe air's serenity and know that we are safe and truly well. For we ARE and always shall we BE.

Wishing you the sweet recognition of your Greatness and your Blessings as you continue to BE.

With the first eyes you were given, you could only see variations of light, not objects to judge. You knew only one truth: Creation. Then, this world taught you to see categories, and values for those categories. Your suffering arrived with your new vision. Before, you were a butterfly free in an endless sea of sky. Then, socialized by socialized souls, you lost track of your soul, which was Love. Love, of which we can only keep track by seeing the singular Glory of Creation: The Oneness that is lost the moment we see "two."

And now you are ready to be fitted with new eyes, really your first eyes, the ones that gave you awe and wonder, joy and levity, splendor and mystery. Today we celebrate your Seeing. Congratulations on your new vision. Cheers to your newborn reason for Peace, for your soul rivers open absolutely to Love once more. May you never not see this Indivisible Creation again.

If you are in Love with beauty, why spend so much time pondering ugliness? If you are devoted to Divinity, why be consumed with the world's soulless attractions? If you cherish happiness, why languish in pain? Build a way out of that place with the spirit you choose.

Our own suffering has as much to do with judging others and ourselves as it does anything else. Grow out of judging and into humility, a pure atmosphere filled with the air of compassion and surrender. Open your new storefront where you offer only Grace. Hang a banner that says, "No categories here. Only Union." Watch as the children come running for the Goodness you offer. Children will always come first. Then, slowly, the "grown" folks, reckoning with the growing they have left to do.

Be the one place in your community where others know they can reliably find the kindness they so desperately need. Be the beauty you were born to be.

Do you really believe you are not a miracle? You are made of the very matter that once journeyed the universe. Water courses through you that coursed through mountains, redwoods, and the belly of earth. You breathe air the ancestors breathed. Your DNA is the precise expression of the emotional moments lived by so many humans before you. Your mind is a highway laid down by nearly Infinite prior human thoughts and challenges. Your persona was crafted by Genius, tailored exactly for your time and role on Earth.

And your spirit... Your spirit will never be measured or completely known by humankind, for it is a mystic spark of light burning in a boundless Aura. And you are the unexplainable Phenomenon meant to walk this world and set that spirit free.

You could not have been predicted. You are unrepeatable. What a brown bear gives birth to is also a brown bear. What Miracle gives birth to is also a miracle. Miracle gave birth to you. Deduce your true identity and live it. Let us behold the entire, fullest Glory of who you really are.

○

Please stop whatever you are doing. Cancel all your darting thoughts. Inhale, exhale, and let this cup of friendship spirit be poured into you...

You, Soul, are glory and light and beauty walking as human, breathing as wind, smiling as sun, blessing as rain, fertilizing as earth, remembering as ancestor. You share the walk and wisdom of the grandmothers, the grandfathers, y los pobrecitos que tienen hambre (the poor little ones who hunger). Let you and I hold this circle and stay in light born of shadow, and talk true talk from the heart well and the soul river, so that what we pour out may flood this arid valley and new life may rise at the speed of bamboo stalk and run amok.

You are not who you think you are. Something greater crouches beneath your skin of identity, waiting to pounce like a predator on the prey that is your *SO FAR*, killing it without ceremony on the hot savannah, so the soft carcass may fertilize the ground beneath your *UP TO NOW*. And then, and then, all the rest of you comes pouring out, comes fountaining into day on a current of your *Giftedness*.

Please do not be mistaken. You are taller than any living mountain, deeper than sea stacked on a thousand seas. You contain all our memories, our entire scroll of epiphanies. You are the inert ash made fire, living as ember, sweet and humble grace on the verge of exploding into a sky of dreaming.

When sacredness was born, that was you. Now we bow to the Divine bird flock in your unending aviary who wing their way daily into your unbridled way of being *you*. Dear Soul, yes you... We are honored to be among your wild grass, beneath your canopy of ancient trees, within your sea of soul, upon the dewy petal of your flower, along the curvature of your river, buried in the earth of your heart, where your beat of Love comforts us... generationally.

Blessed be the Giving souls, for in their compassion they shall be touched by the dew of Grace. Behold the window through which the dove of Peace arrives: the opening of the human heart. Caring is not an act of charity but the completion of being human. The orchard of life is service. A smile shared with a suffering soul. Reassuring a frightened child. Opening our life to poverty, homelessness, the desecration of women and children. Opening by letting our full heart of caring be touched. Touched into movement. Resolve. Immersion into those deep waters even without a plan.

The orchard of service bears many fruits. One being the flight of our own suffering, dust grain by dust grain, out the same window through which caring arrives. If you are arid, open your heart. If you thirst, open your heart. If you fear, open your heart. Let the dew of Grace reach you. Today, open your heart.

What appears at sunset to be sunlight going away is only the sun being circled. Your own sunlight can also seem to disappear. Yet with the distance and perspective of spiritual sight you see that you are only on a journey, circling the Source of your life and joy. Do not be disheartened at the visitations of pain and suffering. They are landmarks on the path you walk deeper into Peace. You can learn to greet them and be greeted by them, warmly and with gentleness, as you continue walking by.

You are a meadow burgeoning with nubile energy, waiting to be touched by spring and explode with beauty. Spring is always with you and around you. Circle it when you can. Even better, dive inside and become your own ever-blossoming springtime.

You crave what is pure, and so you must be
Purity. As a hatchling from the sea, you want
back in your original water. So much noise here, so
much commotion. Thankfully, you are what you
crave. You can have it by coming back to yourself.
Life can cause us to drift away from our center.
Spirit is the wind that carries us back. Silence and
stillness stir that wind, and surely in your case, so
too the music of your soul: Whatever moves you.
Spend a moment with that Purity. After all, you
come from It.

It wants you back.

O

So many ancestors lived their lives just so you could be their next ambassador in this world. Not a bad assignment, to have the chance to live out so many hopes and dreams! To say to the world: "I am the fruit of a multitude of generations." And what prime fruit you must be. So much Goodness and Giftedness are concentrated in you. Please understand, this life, your life, is your moment on the tree. You are ripe and ready, so full of sweetness and blessing. All that is left is for you to take a taste and believe. A whole world hungers for what you have to offer.

Maybe Peace has been given a bad rap. We think of it as a nice idea, or a distant star to gaze at and yearn for. Something fantastical and not worth the attention of more serious matters. Time for a new image! Peace is the spirit stone in our belly waiting to be dissolved into Fulfillment. The blood of vitality packed into our heart, looking for release. It is our highest state, our most intrinsic makeup. Peace is not an outsider, looking to get in. It is an insider, looking to get out. We don't use it enough, to the point that we have forgotten that we have it.

But you... you have an inkling, a notion. A sense of your Sacred asset. You know that Peace is not a thing to go and get, but the source within to which you turn. Keep turning. A fountain lives inside of us. Its gurgling clear water speaks one wish to its possessor: "Surrender and jump in! The water feels so good!"

Every day is the summer of your life, warm and rich with new life. Yet you may be wearing heavy clothing: anxiety, fear, doubt, ill will. Throw off that clothing and choose something lighter! Even in tough times we can afford to let our heart be nude, and dress our spirit in summer clothing.

Much of what we dress with emotionally was taught to us by others. Be free of those hand-me-downs! And our thought wardrobe... wow, what a sweet mess! That's okay, your own new personal tailor is in town, and a fashion consultant, too. One works with the needle and thread of Pristine idea. The other with a fashion sense you might call Divine. Your desire for lightness attracted both of them. Now take it easy and let them do their illuminating work!

Once, in ancient times, there lived an old king who had reigned since he was a boy. He had never known what it was to have a wish denied. During one hot and slow moving day, a stranger meandered into the castle, grinning and greeting every soul. The king was taking his daily stroll in the garden. He asked this stranger, "Who are you?"

The stranger replied, "No one, kind sir."

The king was puzzled, and a little off put. "No one? Where are you from?"

"Nowhere," replied the stranger.

"Nowhere? What kind of a visitor are you? You should be bowing to me."

"I would rather lift you up in caring and kindness."

"You dare to disrespect me? I am a king..."

"I would never disrespect you, my friend. It's just that I have traveled a long way with a gift to give to the first person I met who does not know how to be denied. I believe you are the one for whom I was looking."

"A gift? What gift could you have for me? Your hands are empty, your pockets too. And your clothes look as old as the earth on which we stand."

"Dear friend, the gift I have for you cannot be weighed or measured. It is not visible or touchable. Come close, please let me share it with you."

The king was too flustered and confused to keep up his show of anger. He approached the stranger... who gently and simply whispered in his ear:

"I AM LOVE. Receive what I am and you shall know a royalty beyond kings. Deny the false rewards your kingdom has always given you. Receive what I am and you shall become what I am. Then you too will go walking... for who holds this gift lives only to give this gift away."

M ost of us do not lack in positive thoughts.
We simply need to update our filing system.
Our positive thoughts have a way of drifting
toward the back of our mental aisles and drawers
as we prioritize and use negative thoughts as
though they were top priority missions. Given that
we are our own thought administrator, we have the
privilege and power to reshuffle the deck. The
more often we use a positive thought, the closer it
moves to the front of our filing cabinet. Soon, that
thought can't help but spill out into our
consciousness and onto our tongue, every time we
open or awaken our mind.

This renovation process may not seem complex,
primal even. Then again, who said it takes modern
progress to tap into the oldest spark in us? The
spark of Love that wants only to shine, and whose
only mood is Supernatural Positivity.

May your eyes see only Beauty. May your heart know only Love. May your spirit find only Peace. And may your breath be given to bless this world with the Goodness of your soul. You are an ancient scroll just discovered in an ancient desert. All the world has assembled for your first reading. We have never known a language such as yours, or insights such as you possess. Be not shy or timid. Release your story and show us what it means to be you in this world. Enrich us with your pricelessness, for the papyrus and ink that made you existed only to make you. There can be no other scrolls such as you. Unroll your long kept essence and make us literate in your miracle. Be a revelation to the world today.

A Tibetan monk washed his face one morning in a bright, clear stream. Peering into the palms of his hands at the pristine water, he saw his face reflected back to him, and behind that, a Wind Horse grazing in the pasture. Turning around, he looked to see this rare and mystical spirit sent to bless souls with fortune and favor. Nothing tangible was there.

The monk smiled and walked lightly back to his morning chores. He knew what we all would do well to know: Grace and Blessing are always with us, grazing calmly on the moment, even when we, lacking the pure vision granted by an element like water, cannot see that everything is already All Right. Something Powerful has joined you in your moment, right now, today. It grazes and waits to serve you. Know this and be assured.

Take heart! When you feel lost, you are already on your way to being found. For when we grope and grasp in the darkness, we entice the Light, which is a compassionate Spirit only wanting to bring us home.

With your every True desire, your soul is pointing and saying, "That way." Follow.

Doubt and fear are necklaces you wear that attract paralysis. Break those chains and wear the splendid jewelry of Faith. Then see what blessings you attract.

Be a squirrel, hoarding Hope. Be a geyser, giving all your passion away.

Pay attention to what makes you feel safe, then build your life with that.

Grace floods this world, and yet is other worldly. Gratitude is your passport to that Place. Time to renew your travel credentials!

Rub your hands together. Feel that heat? Touch brings heat. Has your soul touched your heart lately? If you would like to warm your heart in this often cold world, fortunately you may always take advantage of your interior space heater: your soul.

Too often we treat our hearts like kites, flying them at a distance in the breeze of worldly soullessness. Like this, our hearts are barely attached to us, and only by a flimsy string. Maybe it would help if we treated our hearts like windows we continuously open to fresh spring air. That air is the soul.

We have been designed as matchmakers, with only a few precious matches to make. Our most blissful moments seem to happen when we say, "My dear heart, I would like to once again introduce you to my closest friend. I am sure you two belong together. It is my great pleasure to introduce you to my soul."

That last breath you just took? Let's try it again. This time inhale as though you have been given permission to swallow a sky full of Peace. Now exhale like a mountain gently blowing all its troubles out across a valley.

When we were babies we breathed with our entire bodies, the same as all other living things. Now we breathe like bandits hiding a crime, or someone swiping a quick slug of gin from a flask at a child's birthday party: All tight, constricted, and stealthy.

Maybe if we became bold and joyful with our breathing, we would become bold and joyful with our living. Either way, it wouldn't hurt to get more oxygen to our brain! Here's to your next breath. May it be free and oh so renewing.

○

Poetry got drunk one night on your essence and wrote this Love letter to you:

Had I known you were the song bird in my breast, I would have released you long ago. If only someone had told me the blind beggar always smiling without pause was you, I would have poured out all my wealth into your bowl. I had no idea language could be so beautiful. Then your heartbeat composed the Holiest outcry to which I have ever wept. Now I sleep just so that I can dream and drown in the surreal ocean of your words. You are the scent of jasmine on the lips of an angel. The quarry where only birds of paradise grow. Clouds envy your movement and lightness. Music's only point is to be heard by you. Rainbows don't come from rain; they come from the dazzling array of your inner life.

All of this is true. And yet, when you look in the mirror, too often you see only weeds and blemish. Clean your looking glass and look again. Let me reveal how your true beauty makes even Beauty more beautiful.

Maybe you underestimate the effect your presence has on the world. When you are in a good state... even animals turn toward you, like sunflower faces following the sky. Your energy and spirit emit a unique warmth and brightness that people associate only with you. Your intelligence is a vast conspiracy of freshness and originality. Your humor cuts through jungles of tension in a single goofy burst. And your heart is a solar power. When you let yourself be melted, you melt all things.

Let's face it: Your persona is a world changer. It only seems sometimes like the world barely notices. That's because the bulk of your influence is like the belly of an iceberg: not visible on the surface, yet making the whole ocean swell and rise sure enough. No doubt about it... Divinity is up to something legendary when it comes to you.

If you could clearly hear the voice of your soul, what would it be saying? Maybe something like:

"I wanted to talk with you last night, but you were sleeping. So I left you the best part of me to look after when you awakened in the morning. I've just been wanting you to know how much you mean to me. No one else can fulfill me. Only you. No one knows me like you do. You're the only one who ever listens to me. The only one who cares enough to give me the medicine I need, the nutrition I require, and the Peace for which I yearn.

I'm not saying you're the perfect caretaker, just the perfect one for me. Actually, I cannot imagine this life without you. You are the most beautiful creation I could ever imagine. This world doesn't know you as I do. To me, you are a miracle. I don't need anything else. Only you. But oh, how I need you. Today, I hope you will be so kind as to spend lots of time with me. I promise: You will be rewarded... Awesomely.

Your heart is a hibiscus blossom drawing the attention of both a hummingbird and a butterfly. Your heart must be beautiful to draw such wondrous creatures. Some might ask you to portion out your sweetness, reasoning that you don't have enough nectar for both the hummingbird and butterfly, only one of them. Yet you know the truth about why these two spirits have come to you. They know it too. They come because they know you would never offer your nectar on a first come first serve basis. You can't help but share your sweetness with whomever arrives.

In this world, sometimes a suffering soul comes dressed as a hummingbird; and someone in despair approaches looking like a butterfly. You might not realize this until the needful ones get close enough to reveal their truth. Don't wait for that. Just keep pouring out your sweetness and know that whoever arrives must be so very thirsty for what only you may provide.

Your spirit wants open spaces. Fear shuts you in. From birth to passing, we exist inside this vortex of tensions, erecting categories, conceiving tribes, then suffocating immediately as the enclosure gates swing shut.

Each of us is a spirit region containing a wild mare and stallion, their coats glistening and beautiful, who snort and buck and run for freedom against the wishes of our fright.

We are the culprit responsible for the orchard being bare. The soul garden pushes out fruit. Anxiety rejects the crop and goes on wailing through the night. What breathes for a living will never take kindly to the corking of its Divine carafe. A Lover is that which opens its mouth for a kiss. Misery is the one who sews those lips closed. Springtime opens its mouth faithfully and with passion. Which of us will dare to make spring's nature our way of being? Who will uncork the bottle and taste what life can be like... a life sweetened in the Openness that calls to us like a Lover from outside the fortress walls.

A young girl is playing in a forest meadow, dancing in shafts of sunlight and chasing butterflies. She is the happiest she has ever been. From the trees steps her parent, who gently says, "Honey, it is time to go."

Today has a wish for you. May you be the happiest you have ever been. May no one step into your happy space and tell you it is time to go. And most of all, if someone does, may you never listen!

A useful man sits one day, all day long, under a fig tree, stuffing his belly on delicious figs. He savors every bite, smacking his lips and licking his fingers. His body is laid out in a state of supreme relaxation. His face could not carry a more contented expression. A not so useful man wanders by in the evening, and seeing the useful man devouring figs and not moving an inch, asks in consternation, "I thought you were a useful man. How can you be useful when you have not moved an inch all day, and all you are doing is eating figs?"

The useful man pauses from his feast and replies, "My Brother, I came to this tree looking for something useful to do. Instead of tending to the tree with clippers or water, I decided to let the tree tell me how I could be useful. I came close, and I asked sincerely.

The tree whispered, "Thank you for asking. Nobody ever does. In fact, I am heavy with this great load of figs. Could you please relieve me of my weight, so that I can begin my growth cycle again?"

"I was happy to oblige. I have found this to be the most pleasant and useful day."

Dear Soul, someone or something is waiting for you today. Waiting for you to ask and then listen. Surely some good fruit will be your reward!

A boy in the desert comes across a well. He does not drink. He approaches a shade tree. He takes no rest. A kind woman offers him fruit. He does not eat. A cricket plays the boy its music. He does not listen. Two falcons play above. He does not look or laugh. A child cries, hoping the boy will have compassion. He does not feel. He has somewhere to go. He is determined. He is sure that when he arrives, all will be well.

One day, he finally arrives. There is nothing to drink. No shade from the sun. Nothing to eat. No music. No playful fun. Nothing to feel.

Today, may you not have somewhere to go. Anticipate no arrival. Simply drink. Rest. Eat. Listen. Look. Laugh. Feel. Do these things, and whatever your desert is, it may transform into an oasis. And all will be well!

Don't you know how great you are? Those ancient trees who have tasted 2,000 years remember you being present at their birth. It was your sunlight that called them from their seed husk, and then from the ground. Galaxy bodies do not orbit each other, they orbit you. The immense force that birthed them seeps out in your smile. Your heart is synchronized to 8 billion drums. 8 billion suns power your every beat.

If you see yourself as small and dim, look inside with different eyes. Your fullest light unleashed would give the sun a sunburn, and make the moon moan itself from a spatial pearl into a surrendered lake of cream. This is not hyperbole. What stands between you and your dreams is your idea of yourself. All the internalized mediocrity and devaluation. Take a deep breath of Truth and see what you have been missing: All of Creation bows down to you. Bow with it, and rise into your Greatness.

Remember your first kiss? Many moments of your life can carry similar sensation. Habitually experiencing the surreal flush of WONDER can be achieved through practice. Tell yourself: "This moment is so new. So miraculous. Such a gift." Even if you believe it is a moment you have lived ten thousand times, no moment can be exactly the same as before.

And so, let wonder, fascination, joy, and awe come spilling out of you with a freedom you have never before allowed yourself. Let the slightest, most subtle moment be your first kiss with that moment. Blush... Lose your breath... Be taken again with the sublimely sweet lips of Life.

A man sweeps his courtyard daily, removing leaves that only return again each morning. A passerby asks him, "Why do you sweep your courtyard each day, only to see it covered in leaves again so soon?"

Smiling, the man responds, "I do not sweep for cleanliness. I sweep to see the clear and smiling face of my courtyard for just a moment. I sweep to say hello."

Life brings many leaves over and again to our state of inner purity. Do not be discouraged. It is always worth the effort to smile and laugh and pray and meditate. To wash your spirit clean. Even if the leaves soon return, at least you have said hello for a moment to your intrinsic purity. What a beautiful face to glimpse.

Smiling monk speaks with compassion to the soul at his side, a soul yearning for a more beautiful life. Smiling Monk speaks these words:

Fear is your master. You keep an astounding flock of sacred doves caged and cornered, even as you wish your sky would fill with birds of Beauty. All that cooing from within, your soundtrack of Being, is your flock wanting to be where it was given wings to reach. Someone has the key to the cage. There is no mystery to this ownership.

Some fateful morning you will wake with a wild idea and climb to the rooftop where you keep your caged flock. Your life will change in that moment. The bur in your soul saddle will become too much to bear any longer. Your hand, feeling like a foreign object, will insert and turn the fateful key. Your sky will fill with a blizzard of doves, and you will know what it feels like to birth your Phenomenal Life.

S un drinks trees from the mirror face of lake and
says *this* of what you are:

Glistening warm river of soul and sound.
Sunflower colored by a delirious Painter with
designs on defacing the world in beauty. Breeze
sewn by God meant to part the skies so Glory can
come running through and turn over all the tables
in this over-arranged gathering. Lantern lit by
legend to cure the disease of rootlessness. The
stirrings on your tongue are the stories of your
ancestors waiting since your conception for you to
speak their heart. You are a miracle upon miracle,
hatched in a moment of miracle, with a sole
purpose:

Wake to this miraculous moment and never sleep
again.

You were created so that you may create. What an awesome power. Many have used this power destructively. All of us have done so at times. And then came you. You with your persistent heart of caring, bleeding your desire for beauty into the crevasses of your life. You with your tender sensitivity that pain tries to turn into hardness. You will not let it.

Actually, you are a Great Resistance, a revolt against coldness. You with your mind that dares to dream and your spirit that has the nerve to want harmony and Peace. What a Glorious force you are. Dipping your soul into unpredictable rivers and springs, just so that you can get soaked in a meaningful life. All so that you can add your story of Hope to our story of Endurance.

Today, Creation waits eagerly for you to join It in this Sacred Creation Dance. Oh... what an Invitation.

What is morning, really, but an unpromised gift of new life? A new sun. New sky. New moments and discoveries. And a fresh breath of being you. If you didn't like yesterday's breath, inhale differently today. Take in different air: people, attitudes, energies. Exhale in a way you have not before: Release worries from a deeper place. Purposeful exhaling can be actual medicine running as soothing wind across your old wounds, breaking up inner scar tissue, transforming your rigidity into a beautiful fluidity.

Since you were fortunate to awaken today, you might as well keep awakening, yes? Into an unprecedented awareness of who you really are. All it takes is stillness and stretching. Just like you did before you got out of bed. Rise and shine!

Some people are funny. They claim not to be into "touchy, feely" things. Except that privately, they are always touching, emotionally. Always feeling. We confuse our ability to suppress our emotions with the idea that our emotions do not exist. The only question is whether we choose to release those emotions beautifully, so that we can put them to the use for which they were made. Don't be the water spout in summer that all the children are gathered around, waiting to be blessed with cooling water that never comes. Don't be the park fountain that the little ones are so excited to play in, but you choose to stay dry.

Be the mischievous geyser who sprays Sacred water everywhere, at any time. Be the waterfall who decides to gush at double capacity. The old fountain who suddenly relives its youthful flow. Tears don't have to be pained. They can also be sweet and full of gratitude. Your heart doesn't agree with or operate according to these strange social regulations about when and how it should feel. In fact, your heart is a delinquent when it comes to staying in school. It just wants to run out of the classroom and down the street. Let it. That's how it was made to learn and grow.

One way of becoming a more beautiful person is to use more beautiful language. The power of language to create our reality is almost always underestimated. Even our thought language perpetuates and recreates who we are, with every word. And surely we bless and pollute the world by virtue of what we choose to release from our lips. Would you pour a child a glass of motor oil instead of milk? And yet we so casually pour out word poison, to ourselves and to others. In our relationships, our language has the most impact. Littering our Love relationships with negative, ugly words is like building a home over a sewer. The outcome is destined to be unfortunate.

You are blessed: You can always beautify the spaces of your life, simply with a word. And with each word flower planted, your spaces become the nature of those flowers. Your spirit is like a newborn, lapping up the milk of your own nutritious language. With your very word, you change your reality. And the world's.

Life is polishing you. Sometimes this kindness feels to you more like a sandpapering. Or a punishment. Surely though, Life is polishing you. Which means you must be a gem, a crystal, something worth massaging continuously and with the ultimate patience. Because you were born a secret, destined to become a revelation.

Your moments are a collection of sand grains in the mouth of an Oyster that wants a pearl inside Its belly. Today, you are clay being turned. Tomorrow, you are a mountain pass carved by a glacier. A masterwork is being done with you. Your part is to surrender to the carving, the painting, the Purpose. You don't have to worry about the point of your life. Life is making Its point through you. Make it easier on yourself: Become the Message.

L et us be clear about Love. Love is not a choice. It is a commandment. A condition of being alive. We believe that we can choose not to Love. In truth, all we are doing is suffocating and obstructing the Love flow in us that is our greatest need and urge. Therefore, to be Loving is simply a choice we make to be healthy and operational. We can say, "I am not going to breathe," and then enact that choice. But then we soon die. We can say, "I am not going to Love," but in fact, we are either Loving or we are dying. We cannot have life without Love.

Which brings us to you! You have this way about you that leaves others wondering whether your true beauty is infinite. You have this way about you that sometimes only hints at the most amazing soul. You have this way about you. You have. This way. This way is Love.

You may have some yard work to do. Throughout your life, family, friends, and others have been littering your ground with all kinds of garbage from the language they speak. Ironically, they have littered your ground with the very same garbage that was first littered onto their ground.

Have you looked closely at the words you think and speak? You did not create these words. You inherited them. Words carrying negative, hurtful spirit. Words that demean yourself and others. Words that ransack the beauty of life and leave it covered in a foul film of ugliness. Words that are poor graffiti blemishing what was once a pristine landscape. Some of the words are obviously toxic. Others are more subtle in the way that they sicken you and those exposed to your tongue.

Fortunately, all it takes is the mental rake of mindfulness, applied daily, to clean away the garbage and renew your pristine language and landscape. Simply pay attention to your words. The poisonous ones are worth throwing away. Isn't it time for you to enjoy the yard of your dreams?

When choosing a mate, choose with your soul. Each day, renew your vows. And know that you have many mates to choose beyond your human mate. Every moment, you are being proposed to by emotional mates, thought mates, behavior mates, priority mates, language mates... the list goes on.

Don't just accept their advances because you are excited that someone wants you. Think more highly of yourself. You are a Sacred treasure. You are worthy of only the right mate for you. So choose mates like Peaceful Emotion, Positive Thoughts, Self-Loving Behavior, Spiritual Priority, Holy Language. Use the Divine discernment you came here with: the power to know what is right for YOU. Choose with your soul.

This morning, as you stretch your waking body, hopefully you will stretch your waking spirit. Wash it clean in a basin of purification. Say to yourself:

Today I will speak only Sacred words... in my mind, throughout my heart, and across my lips. Today I will reject the seduction of anger, ugliness, prejudice, and judgment. I will devote my life in this place between sunrise and moonrise to practicing new habits that lift me to new altitudes of Beauty and Lovingness. I will mend my heart with a thread and needle of meditation upon Compassion. I will remember why I am here in the world, to be Love... and I will forget the hurtfulness that this world encourages me to be. I will walk the ground of this day with light and Loving footsteps upon Earth, planting seeds of Hope everywhere I go.

Look... something keeps popping up from your soil, persistently. It is a yet delicate sprout that seems to reach for the sun. Maybe you keep cutting it off at the head, or simply neglecting it. The sprout keeps returning. That sprout is your Sacred desire. It is the messenger of your soul. We all have urges, cravings, temptations... often born of fear, insecurity, and habit. And then there is our Sacred desire. This impulse is a good one over which to lose control. If this particular sprout keeps emerging from your soil, let it become a garden. You will not believe how much Beauty blossoms in your life when you let it.

Your garden bows down to you, Great Gardener.

Namasté.

If you are looking for stars in the night sky, but cannot see them through all the pollution, it is good to go and stand somewhere where the air is clear. If you are in the desert and come across clean water, it may be a good idea to drink. And if your life has too much toxicity, when you happen upon something pure and healthy, you might wish to linger awhile. At least long enough to learn how to be pure and healthy. Life is always showing us the way out of our suffering, and the way into our Peace.

Wishing you sweet surrender as you follow the way.

Have you heard the rumors about you? They are saying that you are capable of changing the world, but that you don't even know it. They say you can bless a stranger's day with the power of your smile or an act of kindness. They say you have overcome deep woundedness and have so much more healing to do. They say that by some Divine force, you are able to transform great pain into greater power, and circumstance into opportunity. They say that you are a secret to Peace on Earth that has not yet been whispered, much less sung in praise.

Have you not heard these rumors? Maybe you are traveling in the wrong circles. Look to the mountains, trees, water, sky, birds. They always tell the Truth. Dear Friend, if you are going to believe in the gossip of this world, this would be a good place to start.

Do you remember that first breath you took as a baby? Of course you don't. And yet, you know how to breathe deeply like the first time. It does not matter how long it has been since you have been truly happy. You know how to be happy. It does not matter how long it has been since you have been in Love, or cried joyfully. You know how to Love. You know how to cry joyfully.

Droughts are not reasons for us to disbelieve in rain. They are reasons for us to cherish and prepare for the rain to come again.

Each morning you wake and begin your inner story about the day ahead. Much of this story is a repetition of the thousands of stories you have spun in your life. What if you could birth a new story, completely untouched by your old stories? Would it take you somewhere you have not been before? The beautiful thing about you is that you are a storyteller. The challenging part is that we are not immune to our old stories or those others tell.

Bless you for being a storyteller. May your heart's desires write the fresh new script for your mind to direct and your behavior to act out. May the performance be so moving that you decide to write a new play each morning. The seats are sure to be filled with patrons like Healing, Wonder, Discovery, and Renewal. The sellout streak will never end. And friends will wonder how they can get a phenomenal life like yours.

The first time you told yourself, "I have a reason not to be happy," was the last time you enjoyed unconditional happiness. Let this be the first time you tell yourself, "I have every reason to be deeply happy." It will be the last time your circumstance does not conspire to meet you at the place called Happiness. For our circumstance in life has a way of joining us in solidarity toward whatever we aim our attitude.

You are not just a beautiful person. You are a person choosing to chart a course toward Beauty. You are a bottle in the ocean with a Love letter inside that reads, "I swim a Glorious tide, with no particular destination but Joy." Here's wishing you a reunion with unconditional happiness.

Today, may your heart take to the trees and become a thousand cardinals singing a Glorious song of Praise. May your mind be taken over by a clan of thoughts drunk on *"Being in the moment."* May your behavior surrender to any Puppeteer devoted to pulling the strings on you Loving yourself. May your laughter decide to multiply deep inside like a runaway virus and then blossom forth from you as the beginning of a wildfire epidemic. May your spirit choose to take the day off from worry and instead bathe indulgently in a hot spring of Faith. May your soul get a facial, a massage, and an interior cleansing. And may your day be a dancehall where you break it down to your favorite music, until you are in a full sweat and panting like it's the house party of your dreams.

Once, there lived a sparrow that did not believe it could fly. Even though it saw other sparrows soaring, all that it believed in was being earthbound, and so that is where it remained. One day a crow pounced at the sparrow, startling the sparrow into flight. Before it knew what was happening, the sparrow was soaring. Then, it had no choice but to believe in its power to fly.

Once upon a time there lived a human being who did not believe it could achieve its dreams. We're not saying that human being is you, but please play along! Is there anything you can think of that might startle you into your dreams? Try that. Try it over and over until, before you know it, you find yourself living your dreams. Then you may have no choice but to believe.

Sometimes dreaming can be as simple as this.

A mantra of self-devotion, for you:

I have decided to become a tree. From this day on I will not yearn, but will take my water and sun as they are given. I will live in unbroken communion with my sacred soil, holding fast to my roots. I will stand tall and constant according to my nature, no matter worldly regard for me. I will bow in the wind and be an open heart for what comes to rest or nest in me.

I will not fight the seasons, but drop my leaves in their due time and grow silent when winter bid me rest. I will acquire age in annual rings that display my gaining texture, and I will not shame. I will shade the weary and hold up the weak. I will host an audience of cicada and let them speak. I will not waver before mass opinion nor question my peculiar bloom. Self-consciousness will not know me, for I will be plunged in the pristine currents of being, and will bear no doubt within.

I will not fear. I will be hostage to true Love. I will birth faithful fruit from the bright womb of sanctuary. My wounds will heal into gnarly knots of morph and revelation. Sky will bless my nakedness with the elements that it chooses, and I will seek no shelter. I will not forget my ancestors, assault my neighbors, or offer an offending tongue. I will whistle inside the gusts, laugh by way of the children, and roam richly in the storm. I will cry my sap freely and wear my bark with tenderness. When young Love carves its dreams into my helpless side, I will abide.

I will grow wherever my seed is sprung and let my story beautify me. I will unsheathe my fragrance and release my saplings to their own rendition, my branches never getting in the way. I will not begrudge the saws and axes, nor gnaw against myself when the spiteful ones come to spite me. I will disappear into Love and not be touched.

I will carry my foliage modestly and endure the pride of creatures. In all the noise and noxious grinding, I will remain silent and smiling, my cadence steady and yet not saddled, any harness unthreaded, I will not be addled. I will be Peace. I will be Love. I will be in the chaos, still, and by the moment, as others trade their souls for carnival attractions, I will be still, a tree.

Epiphany: It occurs to me that I have always been a tree. No becoming is necessary, except the dropping of my mental leaves.

We do not speak of Love for the sake of feeling good. Love is a demanding fire in a cold desolation that says to us, "Come closer. Closer still." When it suits us, we approach. Other times we feel that we can afford to stray. Then night comes, and a blossoming of loneliness. Or a June without warmth. Or a heartbeat, curling and fetal, only wanting to be held in affection. Companionship. Kindness. Or just the decency of a smile.

When it suits us, we approach Love's fire. Yet Love is not so easy: "You are not close enough. Jump in." We jump in, terrified that of course we will burn. Then something miraculous happens. The Incandescence we just jumped into is now jumping out from us. We are a fountain of Love, changing our entire reality and those around us.

Finally, we realize that we are fireproof when it comes to Love. The more we Love, the greater the Fire, and the more this world is consumed in something hopeful.

Dear One, do not speak of Love for the sake of feeling good. Speak of It as you would your own breath. You have no choice but to Love. Please, surrender, jump in, be jumped out from. If you want a kinder world, incinerate this one first. With Love.

Young Cherokee takes his daily medicine inside a cave of trees filled with brilliant light. He is a cool brook murmuring sweetly:

When I touch forehead to earth, earth touches its forehead to mine. When I lie on warm ground, earth is a mother cradling my heart in its timeless clay of song. When I walk this unabbreviated world, earth is a carpet woven for my journey. When I fall into dreams, earth plays the flute that sends my dreams to dancing. When I lose my heartbeat, earth is my drum. When I thirst, earth pours me water. When I hunger, earth brings the feast. When I wonder, earth's elements awe me wonderfully.

Who says we are born wanting and wailing? I was born from earth into earth, born fulfilled and never *not* home. Here in Peace and Provision, with a broom of soul, I sweep this sacred sanctuary floor, this earth where I in robes of breath, leaning on a cane of silence, find jars of joy and open them.

The old woman pretends she is a willow swaying in the wind. This is what her swaying speaks:

Do not look for what you yourself are not. And if you *are* what you look for, look no longer. For what you are will always find you. Inner truth calls out persistently to its mate in the world. And that mate, a faithful Lover, always comes seeking its beloved reflection.

Soul is a mirror that wears the singular face of its kindred spirit. For better or for worse, what we contain contains us. What we pour out is poured into us. Our endless inner acres yield what crop we grow. A worldly crop of the same kind, flying swiftly with wings, arrives to our harvest to feed. Flocks of *you*, in the end, will always find you.

Corn descends to consume your corn. Cotton lands softly on your cotton. Carrots fall from sky to spear your carrots. This is how what we are determines what comes to us. Do not go looking for your soul mate if you do not already possess the qualities of the mate you desire. For if you are not those qualities, you might attract what you least want! Instead, appraise and renew your garden. Dreams are fulfilled this way.

What crop we bring to the market, the market has already arranged an eager buyer for. *This* buyer pays with duplicate coin that expands and intensifies the essence of your offering. If you bring a basket of turnips, a truckload of sour roots is going home with you. And if you bring a bounty of sweet grapes, you might as well invite everybody over, for the buyer now pays you in vintage wine, and the party is on at your place tonight.

Be who you are, and suffering will release itself from your grasp, a butterfly that was no more than a nervous fluttering in your fist. Attempt to be who you are not, and suffering will affix itself to you, a bride or groom who takes seriously your chosen vows of matrimony. We each were born to fulfill a singular purpose that no other human ever has had the capacity to achieve. You are the greatest authority there ever was on being *you*. Do not doubt your giftedness.

Chief Crow told us, "In you are natural powers. You already possess everything necessary to become great." This was his way of saying that this external world cannot qualify you to manifest your desires. You are a sacred scroll that no one else may read or translate but you. We are waiting. Turn your holy script into a life that leaves us weeping at the sight of a soul on fire with Beauty, Joy, and Completion.

A mantra on choice, for you:

Today, I want the affluence of my own soul. Give me that luxurious mansion to live inside this day. As this world of mirrors and illusions works like sea against sand to erode my humanity, leaching true union and its compassion sap from my being, let me construct a sanctuary, an oasis inside of moments. Even as mercurial rain of circumstance falls against my mood and state, let me dwell in the only weatherproof dwelling, the place where truth dispels delusion, and despair bows to Peace. Let my breath be a feather from sacred eagle, light as sky, and lifting for the language of Beyond. Beyond this mundane landscape of daily repetition and rushing, where purpose evaporates like mist from the willows.

Let me open wide, now, in *this* moment, and drink what sky offers invisibly. The rain between rains. As one wind blows us toward a life without meaning, let me find a tree with endless roots and hold tight to its trunk, its arboreal drum where my ancestors dance. Today, I choose to disturb the dust of dreariness. Today, I open my chest and release my flock of doves. Today, I want my soul.

If Joy were a giant tree upon whose bark all visitors carved their names, would you too be able to carve, "I Was Here"? If Adventure were a mystic song, would you know its words well enough to sing it? If your own Divine Beauty came to your door, would you recognize it? If Holiness were more than a ritual or traditional word, would you surrender to it? If actual Love cost you all of your ideas of Love, would you choose it? If your soul could whisper to you all that it needed, would you listen? And if this life were your greatest opportunity to know what it means to live, would you take it?

Something great and fortunate has happened for you: Joy is a giant tree. Adventure a mystic song. Your Divine Beauty is always at your door. Holiness is so much more than a ritual or word. Love costs all ideas. Your soul never stops whispering. And this life, YOUR life, is your greatest chance to live.

Bless this day with the Goodness of your heart. May your Beauty rise to the surface and dictate the way you touch all living things. May your solitude be a chamber for peaceful prayers, a garden where you grow serenity and compassion. In your social moments, expose us to your rose blossom and not your thorns. For we are already perforated with sufficient pain, and yearning for kindness and sensitivity.

Whatever ancestors live in you, make them proud. Whatever cultures you manifest, fulfill their majesty. Drink downstream from only Purity and Truth. Eat only the fruit of Gratitude and Humility. Those trees invite the migration of Blessing. Whatever you fear, make it a sand grain you step over on your way to Faith. What you dream, decide to live it. And in the enormity of this Creation, find the most intimate ways to make the whole world feel your Loving soul.

Your heart is a great pumpkin in autumn, begging you to carve it out with a knife of honesty. It wants its seeds and flesh bedded in the earth so that it can live again in a million ways, and feed a billion souls. And it wants a facelift. Hopefully you will carve it with a bright smile, or at least an expression that won't scare all the children away.

Your heart is saying, "Please, look deeply into me. I need your full attention. The hurt you find here, touch it Lovingly. The ugliness... burn it away. And whatever Love I can muster, please, set it free. Do with me what spring does with its beauty. Hold a yard sale and give all my Love away. I will be your prizewinning pumpkin, and you will be the owner of a joyful heart.

E ach day of your life is your Greatest Lover. If
 you are not passionate with it, it will not bear
you Joy or any kind of Peace. It wants your
attention, your sensitivity, your touch. You
claiming to be too busy to spend quality time with
it, this will not fly. Today is being patient with
you. At some point you are going to have to kiss it,
hold its hand, and take it somewhere special.
When you get there, smile warmly at Today and
say, "Have I told you lately how beautiful you are
to me? I am so grateful for you in my life."

Treat Today like this, instead of like a friend with
benefits, and you will be rewarded with blessings
only true Lovers know.

Here you are again, friend. A new day. Life wonders if this is the day you will discover your true nature. Every moment of joy and pain you have lived is bounty swimming in your ocean. Cast your net and bring home dinner. Life is not happening to you. You are happening to life. YOU are the weather system. Change your pattern. Fear is a reflection of your soul's desire. Swing the mirror. These moments are your garden. Put your knees down in Truth and turn the soil. Mind is a seed bag. Choose ideas that will grow into what you wish to be your daily bread.

The songbird outside your window has a soul mate: the songbird inside your soul. What you hear is what you should be singing. Today, become the music you have been longing for.

Your life is your home. Now a mystic property assessor has arrived and has this to say: Open all the windows in this house. Whatever comes in, greet it happily, for it must be better than stale air and tidiness. Rip up the carpeting. Who knows what those old fibers hold. Now is a time for bare feet on earth, dirty dancing. You know, sacred ceremony.

Take off the roof. You believe it is protecting you. Maybe sometimes. Mostly it is keeping you from sun and sky. Moonlight and star shows. Brilliance at its best. And whose idea was it to add on all these rooms? Too much to keep clean. One room is all you need. A center. Stop accumulating clutter. It becomes your master. Spend more time in your garden. Then you won't need external provisions. And finally, landscape your surroundings so that soul water flows in your direction. When it floods your house, you will know your renovation is a grand success.

What your soul yearns for is a sign of what you were made for. Fear and lack of confidence are a misunderstanding of this spiritual truth. If you truly desire a certain quality to your life, it must be true that you already carry the capacity for that quality. This works like gene expression. We are drawn toward that for which we are gifted. Not gifted as in excellence. Gifted as in calling and Purpose.

Separate out your desires rooted in fear and nervous impulse. Follow your soul desires knowing that not only are they possible, they are your Intended destiny. To achieve your true desires is no miracle. You were made for this achievement. The miracle is in your believing. For Faith makes humankind take those first unexplainable steps into Happiness. And we can only create a life that we believe is already within us. Your yearning is all the evidence you will ever need.

The ones who discourage you from your dreams are slave catchers disguised as friends and family and strangers. In Native American sacredness, a Dream Catcher snares your bad dreams and burns them away in morning's sunlight. In the same way, slave catchers snare your dreams of soul desire and burn them away in fear's fire. Those closest to you may Love you, though when they hemorrhage discouragement at you, in that moment they are victims of a hostile takeover. They are not their true spiritual self. They are an imposter sent by generations of human fright to stop you before you do something crazy, like manifesting your dreams.

Do something crazy. Learn to be a fisher of souls who when finding discouragement and doubt in the net, throws that bad catch back into the water, and goes on fishing for dreams. Your truest dreams are inevitably a dream humankind is having. Be the one who brings home the catch that feeds our human hunger.

A bird in the morning seems to be singing for
your sake. Truly it sings because music fills
its soul with desire. Mating call, danger alarm,
social message: all are symphonic movements that
the bird lets out of its inner cage. That you are
blessed by birdsong should be a hint: When we
sing the song within us, even other species receive
the blessing.

You are a rosebud in spring, holding petals and
fragrance. Those beauties are not for you. They are
for the world. You are a summer breeze. An
inconceivable sunrise. Not for your sake, but for
the world's. You need not copyright your song. No
one else can sing it. But you must. It is not for you.
It is for the world. You are a songbird high on a
branch. The world wants to open its windows and
wake to your music. First you must open to your
song. Then you are the music that wakes this
world.

S ome say the soul is a tar pit, burdened with the
remainder of what falls in. Let us say the soul
is a window that never stops opening. Sacred light
has a favored place to congregate. That place is the
soul. Everything requires its own candlewick to
become a brilliant flame. For all that is pure and
beautiful, that candlewick is the soul. When your
spirit says, "I want bliss and illumination," it is
really saying, "I want my soul."

In every moment, say your truest desire. Say your
soul. Say your soul when you are lonely. When
you are weary. When you are lost and afraid.
Suffering is an indicator of how far we have drifted
from our Source and Sacred Center. To find your
way back, do not go running blindly into the
world. Be still, dear friend, and simply...

say your soul.

So much beauty really does exist in this world. Feeling an absence of beauty is much more about not seeing beauty, than about its actual lacking. As you wake and wash your face, have you also washed your eyes? Your spirit eyes, the ones that bring the brilliance of this world into clear focus. Even an encounter with anger can be a Kindness showing us suffering in need, or the direction our compassion should run this day. Every visible thing is a mirror showing us our nature.

When we look deeply, we see the truth of how Beauty lives in and all around us. Work your own blessings: align every mirror so that it shows you Sacredness. Make your day a funhouse where all the mirrors reveal just how beautiful life can be.

Joy must be watered and sung to. It is a flower spirit, a purring persona that responds to our stroke. It is faithful, though it needs us to give it birth, grant it space. Let us open all the windows we keep closed in our minds! Joy needs us to douse it in the poetry of laughter, to braise it in smiles freed without public reason. Behold the bird that rarely flies, and only when all conditions are suitable. That bird is us. Our flight is Joy and for this we have been given immutable wings. What can be mutated is our understanding that we possess wings for flight.

What is Divine within us waits to be celebrated even at the crack of wounding. For even clouds say something about the sun: its presence, absence, and many moods. Only by the sun can we discern clouds as they traipse their forms and shadings across sky stage. Only by Joy do we know the texture of our sorrow. And so, friend, water your phenomenal flower of Joy.

Joy lives! It is not a rare artifact to be extracted from the arid earth of our days. It is not to be encased behind dulled glass in the cabinet, for us to take down and dust off in the finer moments. Joy is the heat cascading out from the flame of our faith in that we can be Joyful. We must tend to the fire of our faith. We must believe that Joy lives in us without pause, even in loss and pain. Even under the foul breath of personal attack and in the wet tide pools of sorrow, Joy is the very nature of our being.

The spirit of life is Joy, an eternal heat of wonder and expansion. When we disbelieve that we can be Joyful, in any moment, we kill the flame that releases Joy's thermal light. Joy can only be released through our self-permission to be Joyful; through our courage to be Joyful in the face of living.

Love is an invisible meadow. Every living thing its flowers. Each of us displays the glory of our variety, some as morning glories, and others as moon flowers. Every face longs for sun in its own way, makes its own arrangement with Light to complement its colors. That frowning one being ugly is not just a person. Remember, you are dealing with one of Love's flowers and this one is wilting. Summon your compassion and offer ugliness a drink. Soon your Love water will be running through another, straightening the stalk, reviving the petals.

As we endure each other we should realize: Some unexplaining wind dropped the seeds of each of us in this same earth meadow, and when we grow thirsty, we all drink from the same cup of sun. When we choose to open our petals and effuse our original, unpolluted fragrance, not only is our own inner heart reinvigorated, the whole wildflower meadow smiles and says, *"That's what we were waiting for."*

Love is the nectar of all true Holy faiths. May you choose a life of drinking and pouring this nectar. Choose to walk in this unbridled place, to breathe this exhilarating air. If they ask your name, tell them: "*Love.*" If they request your title, answer: "*Love.*" If they seek you, require that they venture to Love. If they presume of you, let them presume Love. Oh that your tongue's language be this sacred manna.

What nature Love possesses, may this nature populate your ways. Let Love be the fragrance your persona leaves in its wake. Wish not to exist except distilled as this essence. You cannot afford to be what the world wishes you to be according to its fear, confusion, and collective delusion. You must be what you were born to be, what you were made to be, what you *choose* to be. Surrender to a life such that you are not remembered, only Love.

If your life leaves residue inside human souls, let us pray that such evidence be identified as that most unmistakable luminosity. Love.

Palm trees, ocean, breeze, fountains... all of these tend to move us. Why? Maybe because of the swaying. Our soul responds to motion. Movement in the world. And flow within the soul. We cry, laugh, create, and express ourselves because what is in us wants out. We are not designed to repress, suppress, bottle up. At your precious beginning, you were poured into a bottle called *the body*. That bottle was never intended to sit on a shelf for decades with a cork inserted. At birth, you came with a commandment: Pour back out. Maybe at first you did. How about now? Are you a bold river flooding Earth, not asking for permission?

No wonder we are in a widespread drought. We need more soul floods. Let's start with you. Detonate whatever blocks you: your dams, sand bags, stones. Recruit your community. Get a human chain started to remove the obstructions. The removal tools? Stillness, sharing story, feeling deeply, and letting go... All have good reputations around these parts... this place called Wholeness populated by those who choose to heal.

We are seasonal creatures. New seasons unfold in our lives continually, even within a single day. Our primary human struggle with seasons is that they require us to let go of what belongs to a season passed, and to embrace what comes with a new season at hand. Being creatures of habit and attachment, we often conflict with both of these requirements.

Nature is a good role model for us. Take trees, for instance. Is it time for you to drop certain leaves? Don't be afraid of your own nakedness. It is a form of Freedom, rest, and restoration. Have desires been growing in you that now feel ripe and heavy? Release that fruit. It was never for you. It belongs to those who hunger for the variety that only you may offer.

Are you nocturnal? Let your creativity prowl in the darkness, and have its way with expression's prey. Diurnal? Make daytime your regular fiesta hours. Don't be afraid of daily Joy. Your moods also belong to seasons, not to you. As long as you pay attention to the seasons, you will be in the right mood.

Watch animals and insects. There is a time for play, mating, migration, sleeping, and industry. Don't fight these urges. Go peacefully into your seasons. Graciously bid your expired seasons

Adieu. Your life has a rhythm. Learn its steps and beats. Watch serenity come to you.

Spirit never stops speaking to us. Neither does fear. Those who have abiding Peace are the ones who learn to say NO to the lecherous advances of fear. They say, "Sorry, I don't get involved with your kind," or, "Take your smooth talk on down the street," or, "Do those sorry lines work on other people?"

On the other hand, these Peaceful ones have a great habit of amorous behavior with their Spirit voice. They enjoy the flirtation, go on long walks with it, stay out late, get undressed and sleep with it, and they talk adoringly with Spirit about the life they can't wait to have together.

Two voices live in you. One is an old hustler playing a tired pimp game. Walk away. The other voice is Holy. It comes included with your original packaging. Go with that one. It will lead you to your soul's desire.

Many ancestors live in you. Not their bad behaviors and unhealthy habits. But their soul desires. You are carrying in your spirit basket heaping generations of Divine Intent. Intent not fully realized in the lives of those before you. Now you carry the basket. And when the basket feels heavy? Those flocks of Purpose inside want to be set free. Any discontent you may feel with your life is not just about you. You are but the latest bud on a very old tree. What you want your life to be is an urge rooted in what the tree wants its life to be.

If you cannot muster a reason to bless your life for your own sake, maybe you can bless your life for the tree's sake. Spend time with those roots inside you. They can be very empowering as you continue setting free the yearning birthed so many seasons before your tender heart first said, "I wish..."

Fish tacos may appeal to you, unless you are in a mood for hummus. Or you are a fish. In other words, why consume what you aren't craving, or what goes against your nature? Our mundane suffering often has such roots: We fight against our Divine instinct, in order to please the crowd, or to satisfy our habits. We cannibalize our own Beauty by the way we live, all to serve a mind conditioned by a social fever.

Beavers don't fly, they chew. Rabbits don't slither, they hop. Most animals go with the flow of how they were designed, and thus they have Peace. We were designed to Love... to fulfill our souls with lives lived on Purpose. And yet we fight these designs in almost every moment. Be what you are. If you are a dancer, dance. Singer? Sing. And if you are a Lover, which you must be if you are truly human, then disrobe your heart and let it run passionately into the arms of human need.

Your heart is a flower with infinite petals. If you wish to know your heart more intimately, make it a daily practice to pick those petals one by one and hold them to the light of your own deep reflection. Heart petals replace themselves, so don't worry about leaving your flower bare! Just lose yourself in holding your petals to the light. Whatever is revealed will lead you further into the mystery of your worldly emotions, and the answer to why certain beauty makes you cry. Be a fevered botanist. Stay up all night studying your floral chemistry. When day comes, run down the middle of the street offering your bouquets for free. You might be surprised by how many passing strangers reach out and accept them happily.

Wishing for a lighter heart? Maybe the heaviness you sometimes feel is because you are pregnant. Male, female, it does not matter. If you are human, you are pregnant with uncountable worlds of inspiration: the soul's yearning to express itself. Those you see who seem to exist with a lightness of being, it is because they have given many births. If you are waddling side to side with uncomfortable weight, and your bones hurt, and you crave crazy foods, these may be signs that it is time for you to stop running around nervously! Stop doing. Calm your mind and find your sacred center. Breathe rhythmically. Open up and populate this Earth with the gestated Beauty that Creation fertilized you with before you started wandering.

Give birth to your Glorious signature. Give birth to the afterbirth that is Peace.

When a bamboo stalk begins to mature, its protective sheath falls away. As humans, much of our suffering comes from holding onto our protective ways formed when we were babies: crying, whining, throwing fits, saying, *"Me. Me. Me."*

Along our way to becoming grown, we often fail to realize that we can put away the defenses of childhood and begin to use more fitting tools. For instance, when we are frightened, lonely, hurt, or needful, we can find Peace simply by uncorking our Compassion barrel... Then simply going around to all the human tables pouring out that vintage wine and crying out:

"We. We. We..."

The fragrance of some flowers absolutely melts you. Be those fragrances in the way you live. Extract only the sweetness from life's breath and make it your own essence. Apply it to your skin and let it mix with your chemistry, producing a scent only you can own. No matter the context or occasion, we are all highly sensitive creatures smelling each other so that we can know where safety is, and where Love grows. Make your life so much easier and more bountiful: Become your favorite fragrance and leave your scent on everything you come across. In return, what comes to you will come dreamy and in Love with the essence of your authenticity.

S trange, the effect that a person at Peace has on humans. Some rush to that Peace, wanting to get in on the action. Others are greatly disturbed and threatened. They become consumed with destroying Peace. Both reactions are strong, and both are concerned less with understanding Peace than with controlling it for their purposes.

If you have Peace in you, make sure it has deep roots, and tend them. Being Peace in this world is like being the rarest of animals and then being discovered by a swarm of humanity. Still, being Peace is so much more priceless than being the swarm. And since you actually *are* the rarest creature, you might as well surrender to your enlightened calling. Light your lantern and smile at all that comes for your luminosity.

Serving the suffering of others is a great cure for loneliness. Compassion has a way of tearing down the walls of our home and letting the whole world in. A simple genuine smile for a stranger will do. The soul warmth offered in return from that instantly softened face and those brightened eyes is like striking up a Divine Friendship. A meaningful sense of connection real enough that we want to pour tea with it and stay up all night talking like inebriated philosophers. Reach out... and find yourself reached into. This is the Divine reciprocity and mutuality of caring. Sing to the world the very song you want sung to you.

Mother Teresa was often asked: "Don't you become overwhelmed with this endless ocean of poverty and suffering? How do you manage to stay faithful and keep serving lives? From where do you get your strength and hope?"

She was known to have answered in Greek, pointing to one person in need, and then another: "Ek. Ek. Ek." As if to say: *"From out of that one. From out of that one. From out of that one."*

Dear Friend, if the thought of Loving and caring for the whole world overwhelms you, just start with one. One soul. And then another. For when you Love one soul entirely, with purity and without condition, you are enacting the sunrise of your worldly Loving.

Becoming a more Loving soul always starts with ONE.

Many of us spend life as that insecure child waiting to see if our Loved one likes the gift we have given. We sit frozen in doubt and fear, our entire sense of goodness and worth teetering on the reaction of another to what we have given. This is a tough way to live. Wouldn't it be easier if we believed anything offered from our sincere heart and Divine intuition is the very answer to another's desire?

If in the midst of caring for someone, a fish leaps up into our boat of intuition, maybe we should offer it to that person. Their reaction is not the proof of what they need. Our caring is. So care for all living things. Care so deeply that your heart ripens to the touch. Believe in what your caring wants to offer. Have faith. Somehow you are fulfilling Desire's prophecy.

It does not matter how you dive into the ocean: naked... clothed... with a sombrero and moccasins. If you dive in, you will get wet. So just jump in. It does not make a difference how you become a blessing to others: remembering, forgetting, forgiving, forging... Just jump in. Get wet in Compassion's ocean. We need your Light. Who cares how small and undeserving you feel yourself to be? Grace and Greatness planted the sun inside your soul. Please, friend, stop worrying about method and qualification. Surrender to your sun. Give us your eternal Light.

Peace can be an elusive fish we repeatedly fail to grasp in our two hands, its strong body seeming to dart and dance away just as we feel we have it. This elusive fish we perceive is actually a motionless pearl waiting patiently for us in clear water. Our own grasping is the culprit. It is we who are elusive. We won't stop moving. Won't stop grasping. Won't breathe in stillness, become clear water.

Peace is not to be caught. It is to be found through release. Two currents run in every water. One is despair. The other, remembrance: seeing the true nature of life. A truth that puts despair to rest. A pearl of Peace waits for us. It does not move. Does not evade. When *we* learn stillness and surrender, Peace grasps us. We become the Pearl.

How is your passion today? Have you split the rock of stupor and repetition to let your heart crystals shine in the sun? Have you opened the cage of social acceptability and released your flocks of quirkiness? Clearly you have at least ten acres of wild corn growing inside your soul property. Go ahead, get corny. Kneel on the street and start singing your heart out, as though this very day is your Lover. Cry for no reason, except that you Love to feel your soul in motion. Chase down morose strangers and hug them deeply. Lie on your back and pretend you are floating on your belly in the sky. Laugh at your children the way they laugh at you. Just make sure to let them in on the joke!

Start making plans for all your dreams in life. Then burn those plans like incense sticks and immediately give birth to unplanned dreams. And if all of this seems way over the top, try just this once to *look* over the top. You may be blessed by the sight of herds of your own passion running free.

First, you were Love and Light. Then this world, and your woundedness. First, you were pure Compassion. Then came the coldness of self-protection. First you were flush with wonder. Then came weariness and malaise. First you were a newborn rain shower, enthusiastic and unencumbered, ready for a good soaking. Then came the faint trickle, encumbered by thoughts and the projections of others.

First you were absolute phenomenon, a lightning bug debuting your inspired dance for a dim world. You were a soft bright lotus floating on clear water. The first spider's web of morning, so clear and taut. You were the initial whisper between new Lovers. The fireworks inside their Love. You were the Grand Canyon and its red river. And the magical sheen of moonlight on all things. You were Beautiful. And now? You are learning to become your first self again. This is the best reunion of all: Divine union with your original nature. Hallelujah. Ashé. So let it be...

A Lover waits for Love as morning waits for sunrise. First touch of light on leaf ripples ecstasy through the entire being. Morning is a Lover, too. When Love's light touches our first heart leaf, we know the time for sleeping is over. In this epochal moment—the initial penetration of light—true Lovers wake, open, become an entire new day. For true Lovers, sunrise blooms in every moment, day is born anew continuously, an effervescent flower whose petals are morning light.

One of the first steps toward Peace begins simply... with a breath. Inhaling deeply and exhaling fully are good not only for actual breathing. These acts are symbolic for the practice of taking in what we truly need and releasing what we should. Your life is a product of what you take in and what you release. May you deepen your practice of taking in positive energy, people, and thoughts. May you continue learning to release worry, negativity, and empty preoccupations.

Your days are a garden entirely defined by what you sow and weed out. This is the beauty of your life. No matter what has happened before, you are the gardener of your reality. You have the freedom and the power to transform your living into the beauty you desire. Inhale what is beautiful. Exhale what is not. Practice. Be patient and forgiving of yourself. In time, watch as light shines in new places within you. Behold what it means to ascend into joy and shed your dreary layers. If winter's cold can become spring's budding and then summer's brilliance, you can become purified and painted wondrously. Breathe your way there...

Your soul is rowing across a great lake, moving by the moment for a shore that cannot be named. Towering mountains ring this lake, as do lush forests of tall trees filled with birdsong and breeze. Your soul yearns. What it yearns for are the experiences that will bring it to the far shore. When you follow this yearning, you move in the shore's direction. When you confuse this yearning with those desires produced by your emotional illusions, you row away from this mystic shore of your destiny.

In plain terms: Find the breeze that carries you where you were born to be. Learn the difference between this breeze and those sent by your fears, wounds, and insecurities. Find the inner breeze that lifts you and draft it. Row your soul across the silent waters of your stillness, allowing all distractions to go their own way. Stay true to your way. As you do, notice that you can continuously arrive at your mystic shore. The sensation feels like your heart kissed open by sunlight, washed through by enchantment. With each arrival, learn the terrain so you may return in the next moment. Leave the driftwood alone and focus on the sublime current that causes all things to drift.

Your soul is rowing across a great lake. Before you are a lifetime of endless shores. Breathe deeply and row your boat.

You are sacred. Often you may not feel this way. The world may not see your sacredness and so you yourself give away your sense of it. The truth is, whatever you see as sacred has a way of becoming sacred. Rather, its intrinsic sacredness comes out from hiding under your sacred gaze. Turn this gaze on yourself and see how you transform. Your thoughts, attitudes, feelings, and choices... all take on a tone of preciousness. All that you are and do becomes tenderer, gentler, more Loving. Like a downy feather aloft in morning's rising breath.

We do not have to be as hard and harsh as this life has made us. We can treat ourselves with a kinder touch and see that even in an often insensitive world, we are not only okay, we are better off being Loving to ourselves. May you practice making your every act and thought and feeling a sacred one. You will recognize sacredness by the way it scatters all that is meaningless and invites in all that is meaningful. Like unwelcome company leaving your home and a breeze laced with sweet blossoms entering through your windows.

Enjoy your sacredness. See how it is truly possible to carry this purity through the day, and how it leaves you feeling human again.

Maybe it is time to call a truce on being anxious. How exactly has it benefited you? The tasks lined up day to day are done just as quickly and with more joy when you are free of your anxieties. The eventualities that approach... always arrive and leave with you still standing. Your anxiety has nothing to do with that. Your anxiety has never held up the sky from falling, or protected your heart in any real way.

Faith seems to be a better tool. Faith that you are part of a larger Turning, a force that has more experience than you, far better eyesight and long term vision, and immeasurable capacity to deliver on the things you believe anxiety will deliver to you. Let's call a truce on worry and consternation. Let your mind and body be flooded with Ease and Calm. Watch how your spirit then becomes a paper lantern, willowy lightness, filled with a flame that lifts you.

Behold the skies you travel when filled with Faith, and the bird's eye view that comes with surrendering to the spirit of things. It can be an easier way of living to usher moments into your life through a corridor of Faith. What comes to us that way is less battered and more able to deliver the beauty, meaning, and joy it started its journey with. Be like a flower receiving the sun: Faithful.

How about ending the habit that squeezes joy from the fruit of life, and learning the habit that grants us an unbelievable orchard? The first habit is pessimistic angst. The second habit is optimistic anticipation. Seeds of fulfillment, provision, and sustenance are planted all around you and within you. Trust that the good stuff is already on its way. All you have to do is stand at the door like an inviting host and wave to it.

Every day, you sweep the courtyard of your life, clearing away the leaves that have fallen since your last sweeping. Some days you rise and feel: "*All of this sweeping is useless. The leaves I clear away are only replaced by new ones. What is the point?*" The point is not the leaves that come and go, or the cleanliness of our courtyard. The point is in how we go about sweeping. Waking... getting dressed... eating, driving, working, interacting, cleaning, fixing, traveling, returning... all are circles we travel daily or over time. We can make adjustments to our circles, end some, begin others. Though we will always be living in circles.

Human fulfillment may be found in the spirit we choose for our circular existence. Today, every task and moment is a courtyard for your sweeping. May you sing or whistle while you sweep. May you smile and fall into the moment with a lightness that lets go of other moments and tasks. Sweep because you are alive and able to sweep. Sweep patiently, as though you are giving a Loved one a greatly needed massage. Sweep with a deep savoring, as though no leaves will ever fall again. And when you are done, anticipate the next sweeping with the joy of a Labrador who has just retrieved its owner's stick for the hundredth time and can't wait for one hundred and one.

Your life is a river, always flowing toward an ocean called fulfillment. What fulfills you may be clear to you, or may be a mystery. Creating your fulfilled life is a mystic project no matter what path you take. Mystic because you cannot completely control what happens. And your various arrivals are inevitably not quite what you expected. You take off at morning for that mountain peak on the horizon, thinking it to be a great destination. Before noon you have already become distracted by a meadow. You choose to lie down in it and stare at the sky. That's when you realize: *"Today the sky was meant to be my destination."*

Relationships can be a similar journey. They take us unanticipated places. And so, how do we reach fulfillment? By not reaching. Your spirit does not want linear projects. It wants this moment. And it wants it completely. Your fulfilling life is not outside of you. It exists in you and waits for your attention. It waits for you to smile at fear and walk through its curtain. It waits for you to breathe fully and laugh deeply. It waits for you to remember that day when you were a child, lying in a meadow, lost in the sky.

May you get in touch with your river, and instead of directing it, release it Lovingly. It will find its own way to the ocean. Where *you* may become those wider waters...

and be filled.

What is the gospel of a river? Surely it flows toward something greater, free of ideas and soaked in Truth. May you flow like this, a runaway soul in Love with forgetting, frosted with air, singing hymns of union along your daily movement. Beneath what cathedral does a mountain pray? Certainly beneath an endless expanse, unknowing of boundary, windows open wide, formless, whispering, ever majestic... roofed in silence, walled in Light. Might this be your cathedral, too?

Cloak your existence in bright clouds, fresh atmospheres blessing your soul dance with a Glory rhythm you stay inside of in every moment. When a doe sips morning water from a fallen leaf, what scripture is she drinking? Drink that water, too. Let the words be dew sprung from sunrise's sublime sermon, raindrops purified by a fall through the heights of paradise. Read the words slowly, like moisture moves down the neck of an orchid. Drink the words peacefully... cradle them like a new mother. Live like this today. Your hair woven silk in a corona of sun, your face a splendid fantasy.

May the lightness of your spirit inspire a global levitation.

S ome souls express their beauty by painting.
Others with poetry. Some by simply smiling,
with their whole face, and their entire being.
However you choose to breathe your beauty into
this world, may you always remember that being
Divinely beautiful is what you are here for. All else
is a distraction. An illusion. You are a particular
gift. Unwrap yourself. Your soul is meant to reveal
its preciousness through being naked. Take off
your clothes. Shy, fearful crouching and hiding
serves no one. Least of all yourself.

We aren't talking cosmetic beauty here. This is
about the part of you so ancient that it precedes
human fashion. You carry the first sparks of light
in your generational belly. Start a fire. Light up
this dim world by reaching inside for what comes
alive in you when you are feeling safe and inspired.
Bring it out and give it away with a passionate
fever. Hand it all over. This isn't a time for
hoarding. Each moment is a finality for the human
soul, which waits for your blessing.

Treat your beauty as though you have arrived at a
crisis of ugliness, and you are the only one who can
save the day. Because you can. Paint your beauty.
Donate it in basketfuls of kindness. Don't bother
with compensation. Just stay so immersed in being
beautiful that you no longer notice the possibility

of being anything else. Resign from all other vocations. Catch a charter flight to Beautiful. Disappear into your magnificence.

B less the hearts of those who project their fears and traumas onto their idea of you. Remember, they are only imagining you. You, on the other hand, know your truth.

The essential traditional Yurok Indian law is: *BE TRUE TO YOURSELF*. This is so powerful an achievement that no other laws are required. For in being true, we perceive, think, act, feel, react, and choose in all the ways that honor our life and the lives of others. Take inventory on how many seeds have been planted in your soul by others who have told you: "Don't go down that path." Your soul wants exactly that path. And yet, years of accumulated doubt seeds and fear weeds have constricted your Faith and courage, your passion and fire. So you bend to the will of the masses, who themselves are victims of generational fear.

Fortunately, you are a mystic gardener with a sacred rake: the power to transform your mentality and spirit by will and practice. Now you can begin turning over your soil, extracting those deceitful seeds, uprooting those insidious weeds. Your hands are full with seeds of Love, Hope, Faith, Passion, Joy, and Ecstasy. Drop those seeds. Kneel and plant them. Water them with nurturing thoughts and feelings. Get botanical with your spiritual makeover! You've been given all that you

need for free. Conditions are ideal for your revival.
You are alive. That is the condition.

So when you reach a fork in the road and one path
leads in the direction of your deepest yearning...

Go that way.

A monarch butterfly is drawn to milkweed, a sweet enticement that inspires a migration of thousands of miles. Your heart is naturally drawn to its own particular sweetness. If you let it catch and learn the scent of Peace, it will follow just as faithfully as a monarch, migrating with the seasons of life just so it can keep tasting Peace. Whereas some hearts follow misery, your heart is primed to be a butterfly heart. Roosting in Peace trees. Drinking from Serenity waters. Drying its wings in Tranquility sun. Reproducing on branches of Quietude.

When your heart becomes *this* Peace-full, it overflows into other hearts, reproducing itself. Now you have a proper swarm of butterflies! A kaleidoscope of wide-open hearts, fluttering toward Goodness gardens, attracted by the aura bestowed where Peace gathers. Let your butterfly heart intoxicate on the sweet milk present even in difficult moments, pooled even in the pores of difficult people. Let your monarch open its chambers all the way, bat its wings deliriously, and migrate the entire world, just for a single taste of the milk that makes life on Earth worth living... the milk sugared with Love... the supernatural milk of Peace.

In the American Indian communities of northern New Mexico exists a tradition called Feast Day, an sacred occasion for ceremonial dance, communal feasting, and celebration of community. In one Feast Day tradition, the entire Pueblo Indian community moves as a sea of souls from home to home. The family of each home gathers on their rooftop. All the generations are present. In an act of Grace, oneness, and reciprocity, each family member joyfully throws their stores of food and drink and other useful items down to the crowd below. The crowd roars and bustles to receive the offering. The host family knows something fundamental to their culture: They are not giving their provisions away. Rather, they are sharing them with the community that will in turn pour even more back into their lives.

Then, wave after wave of the crowd is invited into the family's home. They wait along the walls until the group before them has finished eating. Then they take their place. The host family keeps the food and drink coming. The long table is always full. And even as the guests fill their bellies, they are urged continuously by the hosts: "*Eat plenty. Eat plenty...*"

You and I can make each day a feast day. An open invitation to the human community to surround our home of soul so that we may pour our provisions out to the masses. We can redefine what we feel is ours to keep and ours to give. We can gather our ancestral generations and be gracious in sharing our Love, kindness, patience, and compassion. Then we can invite the whole pueblo inside the home of our Goodness, where we joyfully serve every single soul, wave after wave, with our meals of hospitality: decency, generosity, and communal bonding. And with each trip to fill our table with bounty for our worldly guests, we too can urge these hungry souls with our Loving appeal: "*Eat plenty.*"

Let's make every day a feast day. So that this world will be a more Sacred place.

Grace is a paradise we do not visit often enough. Grace... that sense of being inside a Great Kindness that bestows our every breath. Before eating, after waking, in the belly of a painful moment, in your lonesomeness, at the cusp of sleep, try saying: *All of this is Grace.* Feel the truth deeply. Repeat the words over and over, a mantra, prayer, chant, meditation. *All of this is Grace.*

If we practice, we can learn to recognize the sensation of Grace's presence. It feels like a sacred breath around us. In us. Pervasive, invisible, a constant atmosphere. Let your tense heart release into Grace's calm hands. Let your runaway thoughts be rounded up and bedded down in Grace's meadow. Learn the feeling of Grace operating in your life, in this moment. Notice its faithfulness to what you need. Not to what you perceive yourself to need. To your actual soulful need.

Friend, you have available to you, for free, the Greatest provider and caretaker that you will ever know. You are going to be wonder-full. In the hands of Grace.

We do not give ourselves permission. To be happy. To be true. To be free in our expression and dreaming. And arrive at our dream. To share Love. To not be hateful or hurtful. To be surrounded by the quality of people for whom we yearn. To forgive. To remember. To go. Return. To reveal our actual self to the world. We do not give ourselves permission.

Somewhere along the way, surely during our early immersion in streams of discipline, judgment, parceling out of reward, conditional approval, powerlessness, voicelessness, absent affirmation... somewhere along this way we construct the boundary and bindings of self-deprivation: *I do not deserve this. I am not worthy. Too much of this is indulgent. This belongs to someone else. I am not ready yet.* This persistent inner whisper holsters our phenomenal life inside a tragic muting.

Among the roots of personal change and transformative life is a simple turning of an invisible key, a mantra that when expressed inwardly and continually alters and opens the infinite possibility of personal freedom and soul fulfillment. Four words:

I GIVE MYSELF PERMISSION.

Remember for a moment the warmth and comfort of placing your face in a Loved one's compassionate chest. Arms around you, a blanket of solace and support saying, *"Hush now, it's going to be all right."* What if we could spend today feeling *that* warm and protected, our guard finally down, our heart in respite care? We can. Here is our recipe: One tablespoon of remembering that we are the Love child of the Greatest Lover: Creation's Breath. We cannot be Loved more than we are at this very instant. The strongest arms are around us. The biggest heart cares for us. Compassion protects us. We are never unseen, never alone, always considered first and foremost. A way has been made for us, and forces gathered for our cause.

Regardless of your faith or faithlessness, just take this tablespoon of remembrance and rest your weariness in the chest and arms of life's Holiness. You are living inside of an unfathomable miracle. Your every need is a delicacy being savored in the mouth of Grace, so that you may in turn be perfectly fed.

One of life's best moments is that flash while sleeping when we realize we can end the nightmare in which we are trapped simply by waking up. First we are stuck inside of a horrifying reality, as vivid as any waking one. Our heart pounding like a mountain-sized drum, head exploding with tension, blood pressure bursting. And then, we realize the doorway: *I can end this now.* That priceless bridge we cross over into full consciousness becomes our great gift of escape from terror. We can't help but wonder: *What would have happened if I had stayed inside that dream and never woken up?*

Friend, you may still be dreaming a nightmare. If you believe you are living your greatest possible joy and peace, imagine waking into a new consciousness where your anxieties and fears evaporate like mist in a summer sky. Where what you thought was calmness loses its hidden tension and becomes truly calm. And your vision stops seeing life as false fragments and illusory separations, and opens its eyes to the truth of Union.

For a lifetime, this world has convinced us that we are truly alive. Someone could say that to a mummy, too. Two wakings are available to us: From sleep to stirred. And stirred to awakened.

The ones who awaken all the way are the ones who tell themselves, no matter what:

There is more to life than this dream I am having. I am a butterfly still inside a chrysalis, thinking it to be freedom. I choose to keep waking. I want fresh air, open sky, and the source of sunlight. I want the sun.

Let's say you fall in Love. Your heart walls dissolve, emotions run out everywhere. Those twin flowers, Euphoria and Ecstasy, bloom like crazy in your spirit garden. Your lightness of being makes white clouds seem heavy. Your control habits incinerate in the fire of your burning. Your soul has finally emerged above ground and run amok.

If this is the state of existence you desire, there is no need to depend on human companionship. Each moment of your life is a potential Love affair. Even the hard moments bring you a bouquet of flowers. You just have to look more deeply to see those gorgeous arrangements. The more you open your heart, the more life becomes the beauty of your dreams.

And if passion is what you want, try kissing the Divine right on Its mouth. See where that leads you. Just don't be surprised if you wake up naked and aching for more of whatever that was that left you feeling like bliss multiplied by Infinity.

As you move out into the world this day, you will encounter those of great physical beauty. These are as plentiful as the ocean's waves and the sand it brings. You will also encounter many beautiful souls. These are less common, though still as numerous as coral. You may also be fortunate to encounter a Great Soul, one who has released its Love entirely. These are pearls of the ocean, rare and shimmering in the deep, where you must also go to recognize them.

Then there are the gems that pearls dream of. Made of pure light and resonating soul. These are meant to be your teacher. You may think these to be exceedingly rare. On the contrary, these gems exist as pervasive beauty dissipated in the deep of deep. To find them, you must dive deeper than the ocean, into the spirit waters that birthed the ocean. Once you arrive, you will find your teachers all around you, a luminescent field of epiphany. An immeasurable Beauty whose face is endless light.

Today, if you choose to be moved by beauty, be a diver. Don't be seduced by ocean's surface waves. Look deeper. The gems that pearls dream of see the pearl in you, and want to teach you how to be priceless.

Dear Friend, if you are a finder of things over which to become anxious, choose a new occupation. For what you are a finder of, you will find. What you are a loser of, you will lose. Have you not heard of the man who was a loser of worries and a finder of joy? His eternal smile gave the sun its name.

And so hold a ceremony and call yourself a new name. If you believe deeply enough in this name, you will become it: *Peace Hoarder. Worry Free. Joy Drummer. Stress Dissolver. Beauty Dancer.* Endeavor to a new purpose in life, and devote yourself to that calling. Choose something that makes your heart smile when you first wake, and your spirit eager to sleep well in anticipation of the next day. Choose something like *Living Light. Blessed Soul. Woman of Grace. Man of Illumination.*

Your spirit wishes for you to recognize its true nature, and forget the long list of names you have internalized at least since birth. Hopefully, you will discover one of your Sacred names. One like...

Worthy of a Phenomenal Life.

A lemon swelling on a tree has no idea that it will end up lemonade or sliced in a glass of tea. It is not dependent upon a supposed fate. It just knows it is supposed to grow and so it does. No doubt, fear, or self-defeating thoughts. A silent secret spills through us in our season on the branch: *You exist, so you are free to grow.* A few souls stop and listen.

Then they become the secret.

A bird on a branch, bending. Moon at night, revealing. What light does on water. Wind against leaves. Sorrow's sweet direction. Circumference of delight. Birth's florescence. The privacy that opens Trust's flower. Life is a distillery. What gets boiled in the vat of moments, journeys through union, reunion, becomes the purity of what gets swallowed by those who Love.

Just as a flower blesses itself with sunlight and pollination by opening, so too do you bless yourself today by joining the Glorious dance of Creation. Humble yourself by jumping into the tide, letting all things become you, as you become all things. Join the purity of life, and you too will be swallowed by Love and come out a flower. Another way of saying it: You are what you eat. Eat all of the world's Divine beauty. Binge and be Beautiful.

The first moments of each new day are a gateway for what our soul becomes next. It is important to make those moments beautiful, to layer the gateway with lush flowering vines, maybe wisteria or Arabian jasmine. Set up your perfume shop early, before the scents from all the garbage dumps of the world intrude. Walk beautifully through that gateway. Stretch and massage your body Lovingly, as you would knead dough for the bread you will serve your Lover. Next, pour that extra virgin olive oil of purified thought gently through your mind. Let it bless your mentality and imagination. Those leftover foul thoughts and feelings from the day before? Serrate them from your being with a knife of prayer, meditation, or disinfecting joy.

Laughter's tongue is always wagging somewhere in you, a beloved pet dog. Take it out for a walk. Let it run wild, no collar or chain. Wash your face in the sink of Grace. Learn the ceremony that invites Peace to inhabit your every molecule and cell, a tidal warmth that erases the sand blemishes of yesterday. Yawn deeply. Oxygenate your groggy passions. Go down to Love's river in your heart. Make sure to clear any obstructions, and chase away the 'negativity engineers' planning to construct a dam there.

Bottle your sweet dreams from last night and use
them for a beauty cream and sadness screen you
apply to your every last and living cell. Now, walk
out into day and show the sun what it means to
shine.

Stillness and Serenity reign in the hearts of those with the courage to let go... of everything. Can we trust that what belongs with us will remain? Or that it may go and return? That what is meant to be elsewhere will drift away, cottonseed in the wind? Can we trust this? Letting go feels like free fall to the uninitiated. To the practitioner, it feels like blissful birth.

We've told ourselves at least a billion exponential times: "I must hold as tightly as possible. It is the only way." It is hard to disbelieve an utterance breathed a billion times. Except by beginning a new song or mantra: "The breath of Peace is in letting go." Patient practice of these words and soon we arrive at 10 billion repetitions. Now we are the breath of Freedom that inspires the world to believe in the power of letting go.

Myths are like an executioner we follow subserviently down into the dungeon, then up to the hanging noose. Truth is a mystical Grand Piano. Once we practice it, we make sacred music that was waiting in the keys all along. Myth says, "You can possess all things." Truth says, "Nothing can be owned." Today, let's play the music that gives birth to surrender and sets us free.

S ometimes, the fresh fruit we seek at the market does not make itself known to us by appearance alone. Then we are required to pick it up and *feel* it. Today, like all days, is an orchard, a vineyard, a fruitful grove. Something perfectly ripe and ready awaits our choosing. Maybe friendship. Maybe a healing conversation. Or a doorway into our next blessing. The only way for us to recognize this readiness is to hold it close and feel it. To do that we have no choice but to slow down enough to touch and be touched. Anxious darting about makes it hard for blessings to reach us. *Stillness. Touch. Be touched.* For as sure as we might squeeze and test today's bounty for its ripeness, today's bounty is also feeling us for our own readiness.

The best fruit goes home with the one who in turn is ready to be picked.

It is good to place certain thoughts on a pyre and burn them. Let the density of what they were turn to ash, then sky. A mental shoreline cleanup project. No volunteers needed. Only those who want to be paid in Peace. Other thoughts deserve burning, too: thoughts whose lips are like a fountain of nectar. Burn these as incense in a teakwood bowl. Let their sweet fragrance get inside all your clothes, your carpet and walls, and especially your eyes. Blinded this way, you might start seeing again. What comes into focus just may be the *SULOCHANA*: the Beautiful Vision you have been looking for.

Remember that hot summer day in childhood when you put your mouth to the garden hose or water spout and dearly anticipated the cooling drink that would bless your thirst? Be *that* desperate and willing to put your mind to a stream of beautiful thoughts. The pristine water will cool you instantly, and last longer on a heart-blistering day. Our thoughts are not inevitable. They are a conspiracy of choice. Choose a conspiracy that has something to do with overturning Pessimism and creating a new world order with one caste level:

ILLUMINATED.

From a distance, that form on a park bench may appear to be two Lovers locked in a close embrace. Or it may look like one suffering soul, arms crossed tight and tense. If you are a Lover, that distant form may appear to be two Lovers. If you are tight and tense, you may see someone who needs to breathe. This life is not as we see it, but as we live it. Our eyes are only contact lenses for the vision that our choice of spirit creates.

Once, there lived a mystic who saw butterflies everywhere he went. One day a child placed her tiny hand on the mystic's heart and felt an amazing sensation: constant fluttering. She asked him why this was. The mystic answered, smiling, "All that I see and encounter is a Beauty so Divine that I am constantly falling in Love. In every single moment, my heart cries out its bliss of union."

Happiness begins by living happily. Then, all the relatives of Happiness arrive out of the woodwork for the family reunion. They've heard there is going to be a piñata, with promised treats inside, and they all want to take a swing. Go ahead, live happily. Send out the invitations. The envelope is this very moment of your life.

A father and young daughter fishing at a lake is one kind of Beauty to behold. Water and trees set the scene to picturesque. Together, parent and child may even take something home for dinner. A father whose daughter *IS* his lake, his place of heart fulfillment and Paradise, this is an even deeper Beauty. For the fishing that goes on in that Love water guarantees a gourmet meal every single time.

Blessed be the child who gets taken fishing. Blessed more greatly still is the child whose heart and soul keep getting caught by the bait that is parental adoration. Such a child grows to be the prize-winning catch.

Each of us is a parent to every child in this world. Not poetically. Actually. They *FEEL* our spirit, no matter how we conceal it, or hide from them. So we might as well get closer to them. All of them. Everywhere. The quickest path to our own joy winds through the woods of a child's heart. Time to get out the fishing rod, pack a lunch, and set out for the endless lake called childhood. A signpost there reads: *SWIMMING ALLOWED. PLEASE FEEL FREE TO DROWN.*

We search for a way to enter Sacred Love.

But Love has no opening.

Love *IS* the opening.

We cannot enter Love.

We must Love...

Then *WE* are the entry.

S oul growth is as slippery as bashful air. Even more. The tighter we grasp, the more it flees. This kind of work is for Lovers only. Who else would walk a hot bed of coals just to get closer to the moon? Who else would climb a burning ladder just to discover what it means to fall? And what other wild yearning would swallow the sun just to be filled with Light?

If these words leave you flushed with anticipation, you may be a Lover, too. If so, you have no choice but to flounder beautifully in the river of your soul as it changes; or rather, as YOU change into your truest state of soul. Enjoy your river. Its waters are known to be so cleansing that even clouds assemble there to bathe.

Paradise. The idea sounds good, but what if we get there and it's not as advertised? The ones who ask this question have already decided long ago not to make the trip. Paradise is for the souls who walk out into night knowing they will rise with the morning sun. Look at your life, for instance. How many times have you dared to step without knowing where you would land? Do you really believe you are not qualified to believe in Paradise on Earth? Your entire life you have basically been saying, "I am going to do this thing and hope for the best."

Good news: The Best is here! Your faith may be rusty. It is not absent. You use it every day. Maybe your faith just needs a little more recognition. Then it would uncurl inside of you and purr like a Siberian Tiger. At that point, you're all good. Paradise is yours. A powerful wild thing that cares nothing for human fears will be forcing you down unapproved paths while your friends and family are triggered into anxious dismay. Ride your tiger. Its range is an exclusive territory that no poachers may ever approach: Paradise.

S o sweet the fragrance after rain. So too our joy after pain. It is a gift when we stand in a difficult moment and allow ourselves to envision the rainbow that will result. We know how this tends to go. We just have trouble believing in it, living in it... the moment. Hope is an underestimated, neglected note, until the music of our life runs sour. Then the one sound we dearly seek is the reverberation that feels like, *"IT'S GOING TO BE ALL RIGHT."*

Nature keeps showing us this music: sunrise after night. Spring after winter. Serenity after storm. We keep ignoring the lesson, until we need it. Then we grow consumed looking for it: *HOPE*. The flower that grows in the shade of tree. Moss in the shadows. Firefly in the awesome dark. What a Grace-filled life we live. Always approaching Beauty even as we struggle through what comes before. Really, we are living inside of an endless Kindness. A mystical pottery wheel that turns our unformed clay into endless Light.

Maybe one day you heard an Inner Voice saying to you: "*Be a warrior,*" and you misheard this as, "*Be a worrier.*" In your obedience, you became a worrier. You fell into the illusion that your worrying is actually helpful. Friend, it is not. Your focus, desire, and action create your beautiful life. Worry is the fungus that grows over surfaces and infiltrates cracks, diminishing what should be beautiful, weakening your foundation.

Time to correct the Word. *Be a warrior.* Blow on the flame of your true spirit so that it grows into a forging fire. Place your fear in that immense heat. Turn it into a spear of Faith. Walk in Faith, not fear. Stand up straight and strong, your own Holiness your puppeteer. Walk like a free horse, regal and sure. Open your chest and breathe like sky.

You know what needs to be done this day. You can feel it. Now do it. Do what a warrior does to make life and home beautiful. Assert your strength. Cast your spear and light. You hold an awesome Power. Be that today. Tomorrow, worry will be a shrinking obsolescence, wilting from your neglect. And the warrior in you? A newborn, strengthened on the milk of your corrected Word, and ready to Walk in Beauty. Be a warrior. Sentry for your own persistent Peace.

Spring is trying to tell us something: *Hey you, do like I do*. New blossoms everywhere. Warming temperatures. Animals and butterflies emerging from their hibernations, getting out on the dance floor. Life has thrown off its winter blanket and is feeling kind of wild. Maybe this should be our cue. Go up to a tree and take notes: *So thiiis is how you blossom*. Kneel next to a jasmine cluster and breathe in deeply. What you smell is the aroma your own words can also make. Sweeten them today so someone can be blessed by your floral perfume. Stop by a park and intend to do nothing but walk and smile. Good medicine.

Spring is a life coach urging us to get in step with the season: *It's time to renovate your emotional living room and update your spiritual wardrobe!* Yard sales are good when what you are getting rid of is your mental junk. It's not that you want someone else to go home with your baggage, though maybe an artist will buy it and create a sculpture that birds flock to see. *Turning trash into beauty...* a good mantra. Or how about something Spring might say: *Wow, it feels great to be living wild and free again.*

Hopefully, you realize that you are a miracle. Even with all the polluted energy in this world, your heart so often remains a white cloud, pure and pristine and yearning to Love. Some days, Loving comes easy, as you are treated well and warmly. Other days, you have to dig deeper to remain in a good place of heart. Day after day, all of these years, you still pour out goodness, caring, and Light. Most fountains would have crumbled by now, their waters long ago dried up. You are the sweet gurgling we run to for a drink of something clean.

Don't forget who and what you are: *Divine*. The hurt and blemishes and mistakes do not define you, they refine you, decorate you. Your essence though, comes from that high mountain plateau where deer sip morning dew and waterfalls have not been touched by humankind. Your true persona is everlasting light, and hope. You are the fragrance after rain. The warmth turtles bathe to on rocks.

One day, a child will remember you, the kind soul who smiled so deeply at her that you made her feel safe again. That's the power you have, even when you feel like you don't. Hopefully, you realize. You are a miracle.

A hummingbird wants to drink your nectar. A lifetime of dreams, visions, hopes, creativity, and inspiration is pooled inside of a giant boulder in your chest. All the good stuff. Encased in a granite called *Fear*. Your entire social world, all of your relations, are suffering a drought that you have the power to cure. They are waiting on your rain to fall. They have been rain dancing since your birth. Sometimes you have obliged, and let your good stuff come out. Everyone was soaked and joyful, splashing in your beauty and brilliance. Too often, though, you have held your good stuff in. Now it sits, pooling. It's okay, though. Remember, who closes the flower can always open it, too.

Try this: the inner whisper that says, *I'm not worthy,* hold it up to the sky each day whenever you can, and let it fly away. It doesn't belong to you. It landed once on you, and you kept it. If you give it permission to go, it will. You have to *feel* your permission deeply though: *Fear and doubt, you aren't mine. Only my inspiration is mine. Now I set you free.* Practice gently. Be patient. Soon you will feel a stretching that feels like tender birth. You were born to blossom. This is not poetry, it is the demanding truth. Open your flower and give this world the beauty it is waiting for.

When no one is looking, choose Love. In the aching hollows of being, choose Love. Before anger's breath and under the shower of sorrows, choose Love. When judged and scorned, forgotten and abandoned, choose Love. In every hallway of consequence and breach of peace, for the sake of all that ever quivers in eternity, surrender every other impulse, unmoor your sacred Light, and, flying at last into the alabaster awning of peace, choose Love.

Our life is a fabric of continuous choices. Be like the delightful woman who hangs her heirloom carpet out in the sun each day, to bless its fibers with fresh air and wildflower fragrance. Bring your choices out into the brilliance of Love and let the dust lift from your existence. Let your days become an ageless and mystic fabric flapping in the most wondrous breeze. Keep your mission and philosophy simple:

Regardless of your circumstance, choose Love.

Don't circle the well, licking your lips. Fall in and drown. Why draw stale water from the tap when you can suckle the spring at its source? If you want happiness, don't just imagine it... unleash the latent joy within. A kite is fine for flying, but not for being air itself. If you want that, drop your baggage of self-idea. Strip down to nothingness, and you will have your air.

If this day is for a new kind of beauty in your life, perhaps you might drop a different kind of seed. Start in your thought garden. Pull out the weeds of lament and woe. They only grow tall and thick because you have not culled them, and because you faithfully serve them your precious water. These interlopers need not be permanent fixtures in your mentality. You are the gardener. Say so and those weeds will be gone. Then choose seeds from the bag marked: I MAKE ALL THINGS NEW. The moment these seeds in your hands touch the soil in your thought garden, listen for the sweet hum. Songbirds are on their way. They've heard rumors of a new place of beauty and wouldn't dare to miss the greatest concert of all time.

If you are not worthy of a beautiful life, you would not have been given breath in the first place. No matter what you have done in this world for which you may have doused Love for yourself, your reason for being here is greater. No matter how many times you have beaten yourself up, or how low you have beaten yourself down, you were designed to be whole again. It is your irrevocable nature. If you fear your sacred Truth, take hold of something stronger than your fear: your desperation to suffer no longer. Turn that desperation into a wild determination to break through fear. If you do not believe you can perform this miracle, it is only because you fail to recognize that *you are the miracle.*

If you are not worthy of a beautiful life, you would not have been given life. Any lesser life for you than beautiful is only a fable, a myth that you maintain mentally. When you decide to blow on that falsity, it will dissolve like mist. It is your mind's creation, meant not to forecast your sorrow but to highlight the opposite promise: the great yearning of your soul for its kindred song of Peace. You are the Beauty waiting inside the bud. Take a cue from springtime and blossom.

Morning dew finds even the smallest blade of grass. So too await the vulnerable souls for our tender kiss of compassion. The little girl, her heart marked by violation, eyes still glimmering with hope. The man and woman, encamped under plastic beneath the bridge, still holding hands in affection. And each of us, in our own way, soft to the touch, eager to be convinced that a stranger carries kind motive on approach, ready to smile widely when doused with joy and beauty.

Without compassion all of this human existence is a robotic masquerade. And yet, when our hearts spring forth glistening morning dew of caring, even the smallest moment between souls is a human miracle.

B low Lovingly a thousand times upon a weed, and see it become a flower. This is also the power we hold to transform our own heart, and the hearts of others.

Paradise is a castaway on a deserted island, waving at you as you fly over in your plane of existence. This rescue mission is simple: First, notice Paradise waving at you. Then land your plane. Let Paradise on board. Take off again, this time fueled by a force that will carry you higher than ever before. Consolidate your emotional and mental portfolios from those scattered and unproductive accounts such as anger, fear, stress, and judgment. Create one account called LOVE. Set up automatic payments from that account to your recipient account called YOUR HEART. See it quickly accrue into an overflow easily transferable to the COLLECTIVE HEART. Now the weeds of your life have become flowers. And you are feeling as light as an aircraft made of breeze.

Life greets us daily with a sublime and reverberating possibility: When we encounter in this fragile world a lesser love contorted by suffering and despair, we must be in that eternal moment the Greater Love.

Even as our ego flinches for shelter inside a defensive or malicious husk, we must not wither. Either we will be washed over by that lesser love, our bright sand dissolved into the dark ocean of disharmony, or we will become the forceful tide, our light washing over despair, drowning it into a sea of ecstasy.

As we tread our kindred roads, crossing paths with human souls, this we must suppose: When we encounter in this fragile world a lesser love, we must be the silken petal and not the thorn of rose.

In such a moment, when tides on earth are turned by our heart's conclusion, we must be the Greater Love.

Every time you strain to know your Purpose... that is you, knocking at the door of your Purpose. It wants to let you in. Your Purpose is not a thing to discover... it has been with you all your life. And when you lament about not knowing your Purpose, what you are really saying is:

I am afraid of becoming who I am.

In those moments, remember... You already *are* what you are afraid of becoming.

Maybe you've been hesitating at the cusp of entering the home that is your Purpose, as though you are a thief or a vagrant breaking and entering, with no right or entitlement to that sacred place. The Truth is, your Purpose is a home that was built just for you. It has all the meaningful features that your soul desires and needs. It is where you belong. You have no need to be homeless and wandering. Your life is the very lease.

Now... take a deep, self-Loving breath... and enter. Grace the dwelling that is your Purpose with the presence that only you can bring.

O

Dawn wakes, smiling. Whatever cave you slept inside last night, wash its walls in laughter, and leave. Abandon sleeping as you go about living.

Two falcons land on the ground before you and brazenly mate, the one on top cape-sweeping the one below in its broad painted wings. You be like this with day. It has accepted your mating call and come to you, willing. Spread your majesty and together make something new that soars.

These bright hours are for becoming, not retreating. Do what a seedling tucked in earth does when touched by warmth:

Emerge.

Model the animals who shed in spring... lose your coat of dormancy. Wet your lips. Gain an appetite for hidden fruit.

Day is a Lover. Open your heart and release your scent that says to yearning Day:

I surrender. Take me.

Wake this day and be warriors. Wake and feel the amber moon in your chest. Your soul is a fire dancer, *leap.* Salmon swim toward spawning, leaping impossible water staircases. Leap like this, with a spirit that will not be denied. All that ails you this day is also your medicine offered to you by a forest of Compassion. Drink. Sully not the waters in complaint or lament. Leave that silt at the bottom for those who choose to be bottom dwellers. Drink the clear water that runs swift. Heal yourself inside Love's tonic. Run like the fawns of spring.

Wake this day your passion. It has hibernated long enough. Bring it out into the sun and let light do what it does to dreams. Wake this day your ancestors, those of blood or spirit who chase you toward your reason. Let their desire for your life lift you on high, warm currents. Be an eagle, not a rodent scurrying for its habitual den. Be what drafts and sees all things. Wake this day your ancient drum. It has been sleeping in your heart. Let your entire soul play a sacred rhythm on drum's awakened face. Let the vibrations fall as ceremonial rain inside your being. Begin to dance, *this is feast day.* Gather your whole village of breath and essence and emotion, and dance in moonlight, dance for spring, dance for new beauty in your life.

Wake this day and be warriors. Wake and feel the amber moon in your chest. Let it pour its glowing molten power through your percolating plains. Let moonflowers grow in your life, sacred stalks of Peace and Stillness whose faces look like you when you are in your groove and floating, lotus caught in Light.

With a single grain of earth, a mountain is born.

Your new life is so very possible.

Pick up a single grain.

Begin.

Sun whispers this secret for the root of happiness:

As you walk through this world, exude yourself in such a way that every living thing you touch...

opens.

A tremendous power lives in you. All that you do in anxiety and nervousness, truly you may do in calmness and Peace.

We have been infected with a generational virus, a false idea that virtually everything is cause for panic and fear. As we cease worshipping these energies as God and begin to believe in the possibility of moving through all of life in a state of Divinely endowed Peace, we become the social example that replicates into a new normal.

Peace is possible because Peace is the always present true nature of Creation. A Grace sky within us even in those moments we tell ourselves it is time to despair. Desperation is an idea of human perception. Peace is Truth, regardless of human recognition. Peace is our nature. Despair our condition.

We have our illusions, and we have the Truth. We can fall into one and perish. We can open into the other and finally be fully alive.

A bright sparrow brings you seeds of joy. First you hear the song of melody, the sweet chirping framed in sunlight. Then you abandon your mind of daily logic and enter an amphitheater of awakening. In this state finally you hear the lyric that your own heart writes in plaintive patience:

"Come and live with me in this present. Your old house does not suit you. Its air is sad and heavy, yet you keep inhabiting it as if it is your Lover. It is not your Lover. It is a cruelness taunting you. It was built for a moment that has long since passed. You are stuffing yourself into pants that you have far outgrown. Get naked and breathe again. Come live with me in this present. Our house together will have fresh water and sunlight pouring through wide windows. There will be a place for you to lie on the floor in the brightness and be drowsy. Silence will be your music. A nice breeze will be your cup of tea. There will be laughter and, outside, children stirring up the leaves.

"Here, take my hand, you do not have far to go. This road has not actual distance. It is a matter of release. Brush is scattered on your forest floor, waiting for you to set it afire. Such dying brings new life. Your mind is the match. Close your eyes... smile... breathe free and strike your Peace."

Sometimes it is good to be in the wind and remember. Let sun reach your skin. Feel bees pollinating Creation. Your feet in the sand. Let your mind go walking. No destination, no map, pure adventure. You, a child running freely! See your mind return to its origin: Silence. A migration instinctive as for a monarch butterfly. Heartbeat slowing, tension leaving, spontaneous laughter unchecked. Sudden tears, no shame, just flowing. Sometimes it is good to go be in the wind, remembering freedom, letting Sky wash through your soul.

A seed drifts, blissfully aloft in the breeze. It comes from something. It will arrive somewhere and belong there. It will grow, blossom, and be fruitful. It has no need to worry. It is secure, for both its roots and its purpose live within. It need not reach for anything. We too can be like this. Free and simply being. Do we realize that we are on a mission? That our life is Supremely Purposeful? With this understanding, we may rest Peacefully as we live.

We are a seed sent from a Great Tree, being carried on a Sacred Wind through a life of Serendipity. Our Home of Belonging already awaits, in each moment. Our fruitfulness is assured as long as we remember our True calling, and our True nature. You are a miraculous seed. If you doubt this, look around you at this Creation and behold what seeds can do.

B e the wine who jumps back into a grape, just so you can have the thrill of surrender back into wine... take *that* ride again: from what hangs from the loom, ripening, to what is dissolved into spirit water so it can be useful in this dry world. Interrupt what the crowd calls *normal living* and all its insane noise, with a rebellious swath of silence. Be the seed who pulls soil over your own cool body, a warm blanket so you may fall into a dream of sprouting and transformation. Then wake to realize you were never dreaming; you have really changed into a wildflower.

Take steaming plates of sunrise over easy to those who ail from inner ugliness. Feed them a miraculous breakfast. Go down to the river, let the water look at its reflection in *you*. You'll have to let your murkiness settle, and allow your clear nature to emerge. Plant trees of harmony and cut down forests of hostility. Destroy those acres forever. Use the fuel to warm your only home, which is your life, and Love: the opulent air inside your rooms waiting with such patience to dance again.

Be these things today, now, before your next breath comes and leaves without a beautiful mission. You are on a fantastic assignment called *Living*. In the midst of it, make sure to see the sights.

○

Sacred is this moment, for it is *this* moment. No other moment can be so imbued with life as the moment that currently *lives*. In the sanctuary of now, this dust drawn prayer:

Blessed be the ground on which you walk. May your steps sew flowers into earth's kind breast. May that fragrance rise and soften circumstance and grant your walking tenderness.

Blessed be the air that blesses your lungs and brings your every cell sweet new life.

Blessed be the thoughts your mind beholds, that they build for you a bridge to your unpronounceable paradise.

Blessed be the attic you open in your vatic mentality, inviting drafts of fresh spring air.

Blessed be the garden you tend deep in your Loving heart. May what there you plant be the seeds of what you desire, that your harvest be composed of that to which your dreams aspire.

Blessed be your true Loving, which is no flame of self-regard but unsurpassable ache for what is holy inside the beloved for which your Loving exhales itself.

Sacred is this moment by virtue of its moment-ness. Sacred is what comes and goes, be it soaked in the eternal throes of the great mystery that would have us expose our bleating heart to wind and sun, and be made raw and new again, in the high rafters, the inseparable, already here and river-blessed mist of mirrors that is our sacredness.

If we spend enough time, in spirit, inside a place of Peace, we begin to take on the qualities of that Peace. Such a space is always available to us, inside of any moment no matter how unsettled or chaotic or frightening. We own a glorious capacity for finding this space, inside of which our very being may relax and expand, like water released from constrictive pipes into the boundlessness of air.

Because we inherently absorb any element in which we are immersed, our wellbeing is both imminently vulnerable and promising. What we fill with is a matter of what we choose to expose ourselves to, including those elements and atmospheres existing in our interior. We are living, breathing medicine bags, capable of reaching into our being and delivering to our minds, bodies, hearts, and spirits the very ingredients we require.

When we meditate our spirit into a space of Peace, our imitative, chameleonic nature begins the work that causes us to resemble the personality of Peace. We become calmer, clearer, freer, more open, and healthier. For surely, Peace has a face, and that face looks like Bliss.

The path to happiness is not a path. We need not travel to where we already are. We need only awaken from our hibernation, and realize that we are already basking in the sunlight of Joy. Even truer, we ARE Joy. Our ailment is that we have forgotten our identity. Bliss is not a state for which to reach. Bliss is the very atmosphere of life. A flower growing in a meadow does not yearn for meadows. It simply grows there, pollinated with meadowness.

We are THIS close to realizing our meadowness. We only need to nurture our mentality to recognize our actual and authentic nature, and then practice believing in that. Through Faith do we manifest our Truth. And in Truth do we complete our desire to be a living, breathing oasis of Joyfulness.

Friend, open are the gates of opportunity. Hope is born with your every breath and pulse. So too are you. For we are truly alive only when in a condition of hopefulness. You currently exist at least in a state of biological aliveness. Free for your taking is a state of spirit liveliness. The difference between the two is vast. And so...

Many prayers flow from Life's heart to you, now in this dawn of your next season and breath: Unto your soul, a wealth of Light. Unto your heart, a bounty of Love. Unto your life, a flood of Grace. May you live in such a way that you become a prayer for all other living things. Your essence, affect, intelligence, and actions all aligned toward the same Compassionate cause: blessing by *being*. And as you *BE* like this, Hope gathers its enterprise within your *being*, and in a miraculous event, you become Hope's fountain, forever gushing the substance that makes humankind feel safe and good in the intimate innerness of our living.

As you go forward, listen to rain, wind, sun, and night. Each will be chanting their own precious mantra of rapture: *You are beautiful. This is why I come to you.* Over and over again their bell chime: *You are beautiful.* They will persist until you believe this such that you *live* beautifully. Then they will only increase their charms. Your eyes will see the world very differently. All that you encounter will be a Love letter written for you. Every person, object, and situation will remind you of your Divinity. Grace will shower you through both kindness and cruelty. And you will smile and say: *All of this is the Compassionate Love that polishes me.*

Enjoy your walk through life's unending gallery of your every admirer. You thought you were appreciating the art on the walls. The art was appreciating you.

You know what Love feels like. It feels like birth. Over and over again the waterfall, the spectacular aegis of new life. A living cascade of potential, a clay jar we carry to the river source... left to fill our vessel all we want, to whatever fullness we choose. When human heart meets new life (a moment born), a vessel has met its bride, its bridegroom. This new Love, this new life is what we make it. For this is a marriage not tethered to human imperfection. It is a matrimony of Creation's child (our Divine passion), with Creation Itself in the form of a new moment.

Our blessings do not come to us in fragmented increments according to our plans and goals. Blessings flow *through* us, a constant stream available if only we would choose to plunge into that water and its continuous birthing of our Hope and Fulfillment, two currents tumbling over one another in sweet union. What you want has already been provided. You are walking through a field of your every soulful desire. Stop searching and experience the wondrous presence of that for which you search.

Here in this newborn day is the cathedral, the temple, the shrine, the mosque, the sacred ground of *Now*. Here is where we meet ourselves and reckon.

Our heart has a gravitational soul mate: that toward which it opens. That light is our own life in *this* very moment. Our heart cannot open in such surrender to what has been or what we imagine will be. Its greatest Love is *this* time, this brevity, this *now*-ness rich with yesterday and ripe for tomorrow's harvesting. And so here is where you make your stand. *Now* is when you change your life in the direction for which you have so long been longing. *Now...* inside *this* pulse of existence. Act. And now again. For thought needs action to be delivered into change. On and on like this until you have created an entire universe of Joy and Wholeness inside of your emotional dimension.

Your transformation speaks in the tongue of Immediacy, and sings an opera of endless acts. The curtain opens... NOW.

All the ancestors gather around the fire of your new day, peering into the flames, eyes affixed, hearts drumming, your song humming in their ears. They wait for what you will do with this fire, this glistening moment. They wait for you to be *you*, to remember *you*, to ascend on courage into your own freedom sky. A new day is not only a surface gift of more days, more chances, more dreams. It is also the output of what the soul dreams, what the mind makes, what our underestimated will excavates.

So dream... brush off your dusty inspiration bowl and fill it with the holy water that is spirit desire. Then drink from it as you would from a fresh coconut while stranded on an island and dying of thirst. For you may truly now be stranded, inside the limbo space between birth and becoming. And you may be dying... to finally live. Crack the shell that holds the fruit and nectar of your fulfillment: the shell of self-denial. Then purse your lips and drink with gluttony.

O

Of all the candles lit across the ages, greatest for our human sake is the undeniable candle of your own life. Of all the years born in time, most pertinent for our existence is this year now born, today, to you.

Nothing created can trespass against your Peace without your invitation. No wind can howl loud enough to drown your song unless you allow your singing to be a whisper. What are we if not the composition of life itself? And if we are this, if we are this majesty, this mystery, this awesome awning, what growling interloper can have us? What predator can stalk and claim us? We are not the frightened cub we once were. We are now. We are this. This life of faith, not fear. This breath of becoming, not succumbing. And you, Dear Soul, are the prophecy of which the old ones dreamed.

Live your life beautifully.

INDEX OF FIRST WORDS

Jaiya John was born and raised in New Mexico, and has lived in various locations, including Nepal. He serves his life purpose through the blessings of faith, family, writing, speaking, and supporting young lives. He is the founder of Soul Water Rising, a global human mission.

Jacqueline V. Richmond and Kent W. Mortensen graciously and skillfully served as editors for *Fresh Peace*.

Jaiya John titles available where books are sold.

To learn more about this and other books by Jaiya John, to order discounted bulk quantities, or to learn about Soul Water Rising's global work, please visit us at:

soulwater.org

jaiyajohn.com

facebook.com/jaiyajohn

itunes (search: jaiya john)

youtube.com/soulwaterrising

@jaiyajohn (instagram & twitter)

To subscribe to our newsletter-journal, SOUL BLOSSOM, please visit soulwater.org. *Soul Blossom* is a literary journal, offering ongoing news of our global human mission; new book release notices; speaking engagement insights; and invited literary contributions. *Soul Blossom* is also a gathering space for the writing and artwork of young people from around the world.

CPSIA information can be obtained
at www.ICGtesting.com
Printed in the USA
BVHW030841070121
596834BV00010B/390

9 780991 640